Community Children:
A Ministry of Hope
and Restoration
for the Street *Dwelling* Child

Community Children:

A Ministry of Hope
and Restoration
for the Street *Dwelling* Child

Greg W. Burch

Community Children:
A Ministry of Hope and Restoration for the Street *Dwelling* Child
By Greg Burch

All Scripture quotations, unless otherwise indicated, are taken from the
Holy Bible, New International Version®. NIV®. Copyright ©1973, 1978,
1984 by the International Bible Society. Used by permission of
Zondervan Publishing House. All rights reserved.

Printed in Colombia

ISBN 958-8201-71-3

DEDICATION

To my wife, Christina
and our two precious children,
Tyler and Kira.

Christina for her support and love
and my children for their ever present
ability to make me smile.

CONTENTS

FOREWORD

ROADMAP TO HEAVEN

I believe the currency of heaven is love. In God's eyes the wealthy are those who have much love: who love others and who are much loved. Jesus points to loving God, our neighbour and ourselves as *the* commands—*the* way to live according to life's designer. Pretty powerful stuff!

In that sense this world is a poor place.

Just look at the lack of love felt by a multitude of kids roaming our cities. The 100 million or so children...yes CHILDREN...who live by scavenging through our rubbish, who sleep on cold hard slabs of concrete hoping nobody discovers them, and who rarely, if ever, feel the comfort of a bath, the tug of a blanket around their chin. Think of the children who huddle in sewers at night to avoid the deadly cold... who wait and wonder if anyone out there cares.

DO YOU...?

What these kids need is more than good policies and programs. They need parents—people, adults, who will remember their names, celebrate their birthdays, know their favourite colours and enjoy taking them to the swings. Children flourish when loved and love takes people.

God called himself the 'father of the fatherless' not the 'constructer of great programs'. He adopted us as 'sons and daughters into his family' not as 'clients or patients into his clinic'. God is a God of love and he seeks to find followers for whom love is important, who will love the unlovely, the hurt and broken and vulnerable, and you'll find no one more so than the children on our streets.

Greg knows this and walks this, which is why you should read his book.

He points to real solutions and presents a real challenge, not only to our prayer closet and our pocket books but to our perception of what matters, of how we engage with the world and what we seek to leave behind.

He firmly believes the church can deal, *must deal*, with the needs of children and he shows us how to begin. Greg might never leave behind much earthly wealth but in God's eyes this boy is rich.

ARE YOU...?

God has not thrown us three shoes asking us to put one on each foot! He has given us a doable task, an achievable mission. For him the children of the street are not a 'problem' but a challenge and an opportunity. His command is clear. Crystal. His power is readily available and with Greg's book in hand you'll know the way.

Let's hit the road! Are you coming...?

—PATRICK MCDONALD
Intl. Director, Viva Network – Together for Children

PREFACE

Why write about children who live on the street? As I sit here at my desk asking myself that question, my mind is filled with hundreds, even thousands of children and youth who have taken to the streets of our cities around the world. Some of the faces are familiar; because they come from the streets of Caracas, others come from Bogotá; Manila; Amsterdam; San José and Los Angeles. God loves these children and knows them each by name.

In 1992, as I sat in chapel at Multnomah Bible College in Portland, Oregon, God spoke to me! He spoke to me through the preaching of Doug Nichols, international director of Action International Ministries. Doug closed the session one evening with a story about a group of boys on the street who had been mistreated. He described to us how someone had stood up and defended the children. He closed with a question, "You can do that, can't you?" "Wow, you mean me Lord?" In the summer of 1992 I was on my way to Bogotá, Colombia to minister to these children that Doug spoke about. After an eye-opening summer of ministry I returned to Multnomah asking myself, "how can I *not* return?" God had worked in my own life during that summer.

In 1993 I was invited to visit Jon and Shannon Haslett in Caracas, Venezuela and their new work among homeless children there. I accepted their invitation and spent three weeks wandering around the country of Venezuela, along with Jon, seeking God for direction about my future and accompanying him as he sought the Lord on where to start a project with homeless youth. We visited with many desperate children and teens during those three weeks and once again, God spoke to me about my future ministry among His children.

After I graduated from Multnomah I began to make preparations to work with *Niños de la Luz* (Children of the Light) in Caracas, Venezuela (the organization founded by Jon and Shannon Haslett). After two remarkable years of work in Caracas I returned to California to begin graduate studies at Fuller Theological Seminary. I arrived at Fuller with a purpose. I wanted to research "street children" and take time to think through my future ministry and how to more effectively reach out and be a catalyst in helping these children transform their lives. This book is the result of my research on such children and youth. Most of the stories that are included here come from those early years of working with the children and youth on the *Sabana Grande* boulevard of Caracas.

Upon graduating from Fuller Seminary, my wife Christina and I joined the Latin America Mission and soon departed for Venezuela to work once again with *Niños de la Luz*. We have been privileged to work with a wonderful staff that is dedicated to bringing hope to the hopeless. *Niños de la Luz* of Venezuela continues to grow and develop into a ministry that is dedicated to reaching homeless and abandoned children on the street for Jesus Christ. The ministry is now lead by a Venezuelan team of committed believers who are devoted to protecting these children.

You should know that most of the children named in the following pages and some places have been altered to protect the children and/or workers.

I would like to especially thank Kathy Clark for her editorial skills. I am also grateful for many others who have shared their words of encouragement and thus moved this book a little closer toward publication. Thanks goes to the *Niños de la Luz* team, both past and present for their friendship and solidarity, and to the boys (and young men) at the Lighthouse Ranch. You have given me much more than I have given you!

It is my prayer that God will use what is written on these pages to encourage you in your own journey to be used of God. For what greater privilege is there than to be used by God in reaching out to His children.

—Greg W. Burch
Caracas, Venezuela

INTRODUCTION

THE CONTEXT

In 1992, while visiting a project working with homeless and abandoned children[1] in Bogotá, Colombia, I heard some of the most devastating words one can hear. One afternoon I was in the downtown area of Bogotá visiting with some children living on the street when a man walked up to me and began to tell me how beautiful a country Colombia was. I was in agreement with him, for Colombia, like its people, is a very beautiful country. Soon our conversation switched to the children that were before us, and his remarks were hateful and disrespectful as he told me that I ought to go see other parts of the country instead of looking at this "trash."

Unfortunately, this man in Colombia is not alone. Many people around the world do not see these children for who they are, as people bearing the image of God. Historically, children living on the street in our world's cities have been called anything from "trash" to "street children." Some names given to children on the street are, vermin, trash, disposable ones, shoe glue inhalers and such things as thieves and criminals (Kilbourn 1997:7-8). One can find among people of every culture particular

---

1- By "children" I refer to those that are under the age of 18. Sometimes the word "youth" will be used for those older children on the street.

derogatory words focused towards the homeless child. What kind of message are we sending to a child when we say, "you are disposable?"

To many, these children are worthless and should be hidden so that they will not bring embarrassment to their country's reputation. The United States government shrinks from admitting that there are 1.1 million children in homeless shelters at any given time (National Coalition for the Homeless). Certainly the Bolivian government does not like to acknowledge that it has 1,500 to 2,000 children sleeping on its streets (Bolivian Government, Census Figures, 1992). Similarly, Brazil is perplexed over how to help the 12 million children on the streets throughout the country (Action International Ministries).

Worldwide the statistics for children living on the streets are conflicting. Some say there are 200 million[2] children living on the street, while others say it is closer to 8 million.[3] Quite a discrepancy! Patrick McDonald, founder and international director of the Viva Network,[4] and many others argue that it is very difficult to actually nail down the number of children living on the street (2000:23). In Guatemala we see a similar trend. The numbers vary from 600 to 5,000 children living on the streets (Tierney 1997:4). We can be certain that one child on the street is one child too many. Realistically, the situation is desperate. "There are an estimated twelve million homeless children on the streets of Brazil. Their parents lost them in the crowds, put them out, or they died. However they go there, they are

---

2- See Reaching Children in Need by Patrick McDonald.
3- UNESCO.
4- The Viva Network is a global movement of Christians that seeks to create and sustain networks of Christian workers working with children at risk.

there. They beg, they steal, they sell their bodies. They eat garbage. They start scared and end scarred, hard, and dead," says John Piper (1997:40). As Piper descriptively writes, the children and young people that we will deal with in this book are living in crisis. They are desperate and are just barely surviving!

The situation in Latin America is surreal. The numbers are just too great to imagine. Many have concluded that there are at least 30 million children on the street, either working or living each day.[5] In other words, some say there are as many children on the street each day as there are people living in Canada. Just as with world statistics, there are also discrepancies among statistics in the Latin American context. This discrepancy is well documented in the research article, "Street children of Juarez" (Lusk et. al. 1989:290-291). These children present one of the biggest welfare issues confronting Latin American nations. (Raffaelli 1997:89).

On a daily basis I see children either working or living on the streets in Caracas. Perhaps they are not so obvious to others in the city. I see them because I am looking for them. That is the difference. Some years ago while on a research trip with my good friend Jon Haslett, founder of the ministry *Niños de la Luz*, we constantly received words like, "no, we don't have that problem here" in response to our questions about children on the street. Children live on the periphery of society. These children who live in the margins of our cities are often difficult to locate. Many of them do not remain in one place for too long and they

---

5- See John G. Cosgrove in "Towards a Working Definition of Street Children."

sleep in abandoned houses and buildings where few people wander. Some children even keep themselves hidden away from mainstream society, not wanting to be seen.

Despite the statistics that we often hear about homeless children, the emphasis throughout this writing is on the individual child. Mother Teresa would often say that ministry to the hurting is about reaching one person at a time—it's one drop in the bucket that eventually fills it up. We must remember the faces, the face of each child that suffers. We are called to reach out to the individual person. There is no short cut here.

1

UNDERSTANDING THE CHILDREN

DEFINING "STREET CHILDREN"

What exactly do people mean when they utter the words "street children"? An early definition for the term "street children" which was proposed by the Inter-NGO Programme for Street Children and Street Youth goes like this: "Street children are those for whom the street (in the widest sense of the word: i.e. unoccupied dwellings, wasteland etc.) more than their family has become their real home, a situation in which there is no protection, supervision or direction from responsible adults (Ennew 2000:14). Cockburn has defined street children as "those who have abandoned their homes, schools and immediate communities, before they are sixteen years of age, and have drifted into a nomadic street life" (1991:12-13). While definitions vary, the basic understanding is that these children are, for the most part, homeless (whether they are runaways or have been abandoned) and on their own on the street without adult supervision. Some children are on the street temporarily while others are there permanently unless there is intervention.

In reality the term "street children" is too general in respect to the children we see in the street. It will be helpful to understand some of the following categories that have been constructed in order to bring some clarity to the general term, "street children."

UNICEF has proposed the following groupings:

- Children at High Risk
- Children in the Street
- Children of the Street

• *Children at High Risk* are seen as boys and girls who live in total poverty. Most of these children are found in slums or squatter villages. Their most basic needs are not met and they are often deprived of even basic education. Many of the children can be found playing and helping out at home with parents absent for most of the day. These children are at high social risk because they are not cared for by an adult and could end up in the next grouping of Children in the Street.

• *Children in the Street* are those children that are found working on the street both day and night. These children make money by selling flowers, candy, balloons, shining shoes, etc. These children might on occasion sleep on the street but continue to have their primary contact with home. These children are no longer in school and have minimal formal education. A 1985 UNICEF report in Quito, Ecuador, found that most of the children were involved in selling food items (61%) while others were shoe shiners (15%). Other children were found to be involved in selling other items, such as souvenirs, roses, and even illegal drugs (14%). This population is quite large and is at risk of developing into Children of the Street.

• *Children of the Street* are those boys and girls that are living on the street with very little contact with home. As mentioned above, these are children that have either been forced to live on the street or have chosen to do so because of an irregular home situation. These children are literally brought up disconnected from the family and the school. Unfortunately many of the young people will eventually become involved with drugs and stealing. Manipulation will become a valuable asset for these young people as well, for their very lives will depend on it.

Another author lists the children in four categories: 1) Totally abandoned children, 2) Partially abandoned children, 3) Street urchins/latch-key children, and 4) Working children (Beaunaux 1996:375). These designations focus on the fact that their parents, either out of necessity or for other reasons, have abandoned their children and youth.

• *Totally abandoned children* are seen as the "children of the street" above. In Colombia they are known as *gamin*, in Brazil, *garoto* and in Mexico, the *pelón*. In Venezuela they are called the "*huelepegas*" a term referring to their habit of inhaling shoe glue fumes. As already mentioned they live primarily on the street with little family contact.

• *Partially abandoned children* are children of the street and children in the street. They spend much time on the street but do not live there full time. They, for the most part, do not work. They soon get into drug use from the other boys and girls who are totally abandoned.

- Street urchins/latch-key kids are those boys and girls that roam the streets but do not loose contact with their homes. They do not use drugs and they do not work on the street.

- Working children are seen as those who have contact with their home. In fact they mostly sleep at home but spend most of their days on the street working. They wash car windows, sell flowers and shine shoes (Beaunaux 1996:375).

Regardless of the typology stated above, one thing is certain, there are a number of different children, each with his or her own story and history roaming the streets of our cities worldwide. While these terms help us in our own categorizing of them, we must not forget that these children and youth are individuals with a tremendous amount of needs.

While most of the children and youth that are referred to from this point forward are considered children of the street or totally abandoned children, there is overlap. The Christian community has been asked by our Lord to be in direct contact with and assistance to those that are destitute and needy. For us to enter into solidarity only with one group is to exclude a large amount of needy children. It is probable that other children, such as those who work in the street during the day (cleaning shoes or selling items), having some contact with their parents, will benefit from some of the following outreaches and ideas.

It should be noted that many organizations make no real distinction between these different groups of children. As we walk with children in need, we must remember the different issues that particular children represent. Many groups of people wanting to help will often "batch process" those children who need assistance (Scanlon, Tomskin, Lynch and Scanlon 1998:7). By "batch processing," what is meant is all children, including those that are working on the street, in the street and of the street are mixed and received into the same program or house. While the sincerity of the groups that batch process is admirable, there is need, I believe, to recognize these children as representing different situations and to work with them accordingly. As we will soon see, context is everything. For example, if a group of children who shine shoes on the street is mixed with older youth living on the street, (i.e. children that beg and steal in order to buy drugs) there will be conflicts. The two groups will most definitely not get along, but it can also lead the older youth into influencing those not yet living on the street.

AN URBAN DILEMMA

Much can be written about our cities' issues and problems, but one must not forget to mention the children that our urban centers harbor. Children are living on the street of most of our world's cities. A few years ago I met with several young people on the streets of Portland, Oregon after a return visit to the U.S. from Venezuela. I was shocked to see young people living on the street in Portland. As we talked on the street corner, two police on horseback approached us and asked what we were doing. Perhaps they thought I, too, was living on the street, for I was not much older than those with whom I was talking. One of the guys said, "we're just hanging out like usual." The police soon left us, not recognizing a threat, I assume. I mentioned to the youth that the police in other countries are not so kind to young people on the street. They were quick to remind me that they are not always received so kindly themselves by the police. The young men were shocked, however, as I told them about the beatings and shootings that some "street kids" receive in different countries.

Many of our cities' leaders are perplexed and do not have a viable answer as to how we might assist young people on the street. Homeless children are a fairly new issue in Bujumbura, Burundi. Whereas some years earlier there were nearly no children living on the street, in 1998 there were close to 20,000 children living there, with most of them receiving no help from NGO's or the government. Urbanization, the AIDS epidemic and armed conflict has sent children into the capital city to survive on its streets.[6] Within Caracas, Venezuela we find an issue that has created our urban dilemma. Many of the rural poor have literally poured into the city in search of jobs and better living conditions only to find cramped housing situations, often having to build on top of another family member's home. Urbanization in Venezuela is currently at eighty-four percent and with an uncertain future the city's growth will only continue. So what happens when a rural family moves to the city and cannot find a job, has no food and is

6- All Africa News Press Service, February 9, 1998.

desperate? The hopelessness and despair will often lead the men to drinking and drugs which in turn leads the women and children to find food and provision. Many of the boys and girls that I meet on the street very often are there because they are sent to the streets to beg. One boy named Luis, was forced out of his home because there simply was not enough food to feed his younger brothers and sisters. Luis tried begging on the street in order to bring home money, but his earnings never seemed to help out that much. He had no other choice than to find his provisions on the street. Soon the street became his home. Many children start their young lives begging to bring home money to help in the home. Little Bizimana in the capital city of Burundi, Bujumbura, collects money and gives part of this to his mother in order to make ends meet.[7]

The percentage of people living in urban shantytowns is staggering! Once again, rural to urban migration is the most likely culprit for why so many have turned to the city as a place of hope, yet what they find is, indeed, hopelessness. Close to 50 percent of the world's population live in urban centers. Most of these people are poor and not yet Christians (Greenway and Monsma 1989:45). The poorest neighborhoods in Caracas and other major places in the Latin world are truly astonishing. Upon entering the city of Caracas the first thing one sees is the massive number of small houses stacked on top of each other, just barely clinging to the hillside. As you enter the heart of the city, it is impossible to lose sight of the small red-bricked houses known as the *"barrios."*

7- All Africa News Press Service, February 9, 1998.

Overcrowding and desperate living situations thrust children into city centers where only despair and hopelessness awaits them. Too few governments are prepared to deal with the numbers of rural migrants arriving in the cities at staggering rates. While some governments seem to be content with their new arrivals, others have begun to push many migrants back to where they came from without much success.[8] Many migrants choose the city in search of hope, for the city indeed represents a place of hope for the suffering. In 1989, Timothy Monsma reported that in Africa, Latin America and Asia, the shantytowns inside of the urban centers were "numerous, populous, and growing" (1989:2). In cities such as Quelimane in Mozambique, urbanization over the years has been sought because of safety issues due to armed conflict. David Vincent of *City Watch* reports that "Quelimane is a port city and the estimated population of 100,000 [1992] has been swollen by an influx of rural dwellers, arriving by road and by sea, and driven by insecurity in the districts, hunger and dire poverty" (1995:2).

Urbanization is only predicted to increase in the future. Some believe that cities will grow at twice the rate of national growth, with large cities growing three to four times as much (Conn and Ortiz: 2001). What does this mean for the children? Children and youth will continue to seek out their own existence on the city streets at an increasing rate if aggressive preventive actions are not

---

8- President Hugo Chávez of Venezuela calls this 'reverse-migration' and is committed to creating incentives for the people to return to the rural and agricultural areas of the south in Venezuela (Gott 2000:12).

taken. By aggressive preventive actions, I mean first recognizing the need and then working with the community to discover solutions to the issue at hand before children are drawn to the street. This action will primarily be dependent upon the Church of God as we thoughtfully and delicately live out our calling to be salt and light in the world (Matthew 5:13-16).

Perhaps an illustration will help clarify the point. I enjoy taking care of plants. I guess you can call me an amateur botanist! The other day while I was watering one of my dear plants in the front room, I noticed that the leaves were becoming more and more droopy, as if someone forgot to water them. I wonder who that could have been? After a few days, my poor plant continued to look as if it needed water. It turned out that some little creatures had discovered my plant tasted good and had begun to devour it. This is where the "amateur" in my interest in botany really comes out, so I went to the local nursery and brought a sample of my poor plant in case I needed help explaining what the problem was. The "professional" botanist knew exactly what the *root cause* was and sent me home with the remedy in a bottle.

Is there a remedy for what's taking place among the children in our urban environments? Unfortunately it is not as simple as a "remedy in a bottle," but yes, of course there is a solution. The solution lies in acknowledging the *root cause* and analyzing this within the framework of the community, the community of God and the local community of the particular child.

IN CONCLUSION

The fact that there are children living on the street is primarily an urban dilemma. Some feel that this is because the social and community pressures are no longer present to safeguard the children from harm. Perhaps this is true. Conflicts and disagreements between children and their parents are often the result of new urban values adopted by these urban children (Conn & Ortiz 2001:21). The fact is, children and youth now make up the majority of city-dwellers. What relevance does this have on our subject? Plenty. It is crucial that we not only recognize that urbanization is taking its toll on the family, but that our urban dwellers are becoming younger. That is why this issue is so important! We must refocus the Church's perspective on children and youth living in new urban environments. We must include the child as Jesus so clearly did in Mark 10:13-16. To include the child is to remember that Christ died for the child and beckons the child to come to Him. No longer must church be primarily an adult event, we must include the child.

At a recent Cutting Edge Conference[9] on children at risk, a new direction in missional theology was presented. Named after its host location, it was referred to as the "Penang Consultation on Child Theology." To this I say Amen! The Church desperately needs to refocus its direction on the child, especially those at-risk

As the city becomes younger, so should our mission

---

* Cutting Edge Conference, held in Dalfsen, Netherlands, October 14-18, 2002. Organized by the Viva Network.

theology. The key to developing a strategy for winning young people in our cities lies in our understanding of God's heart for these children and seeing them for who they are, the children of God.

2

CHILDREN AND COMMUNITY

COMMUNITY CHILDREN

Josué and Héctor, brothers, left their home when they were seven and nine respectively. Their home was filled with nothing but drug addiction and abuse. After several weeks on the street they met up with some Christians who were running a program for people with drug addictions. Even though neither had yet gotten involved with drugs, the leaders of the home decided to take them in and get them off the street. The rehabilitation center was mainly filled with older adolescents and young adults, so the leadership decided to contact us at *Niños de la Luz*.

After several meetings to discuss the family situation of the boys and their future, it was decided that they would be better off if they were at least temporarily in another location, away from home until the family itself could be helped. We invited them to live at the Lighthouse Ranch.

The Lighthouse Ranch is home for a number of "ex-street children" who have chosen to leave the streets behind and join our community. The staff at the Lighthouse is committed to applying kingdom values to everyday life. Within the three homes located on the ranch-like property there are parents and up to eight children being cared for at anytime.

The philosophy behind this approach is that the homes become less institutional and more family oriented. Over the years, numerous Christians attempted to house as many orphans and abandoned children as possible. They sometimes did so by creating large child-care institutions while sacrificing the individuality of the children. Those involved with *Niños de la Luz* believe in the importance of creating family models for the children, who in turn will go on to create their own families. These children were once thought of as "street children" but are now examples to the world that their Heavenly Father cares and delights in seeing these "throwaways" brought under His wings and cared for.

We believe that God wants to use us as a small body of Christians to be an extension of His hands and feet in the lives of these boys. The Lighthouse Ranch is made up of a group of people who believe in the potential of every child and believe that God, the Father of the fatherless, is exceedingly concerned for their well-being. As a team our goal is simply to be guides who love these children unconditionally. Community is what we are all about. Community must be at the heart of all that we do in our outreach to bring hope to hurting young people.

As has already been mentioned, the term "street children" is a common term used for children who either live part of the time on the street or have made the street their home.

To be honest, I am uncomfortable with the category "street children." Thus, as you read on you will notice my usage of "community children." This is intentional. While working, in the past, day and night with children and youth on the streets, I would often refer to them as "street children" or "street kids." The usage of this term has disturbed me, thus I have sought a more appropriate one for others and myself who work with this grouping of children at risk. Recently while doing some research I came across the term "community children." While it is not a perfect term, I have chosen to use it. Some will certainly argue that the term lacks description. I understand this, but I would rather be lacking in my description than simply inaccurate and possibly harmful in my terminology. Some other terms are also possible for these children. For example, street *dwelling* or *living* children are terms that help describe the situation in which they find themselves. These are expressions I will use at times as well. The bottom line is, the dignity of our children obligates us to think carefully about how we refer to them.

Others are concerned about the term as well. Some even find the term "street children" demeaning; notice how Patricia Carol Márquez comments on the usage of the nomenclature: "'Street children' as a general category glosses over the heterogeneity of these young people's lives, depriving them of individuality" (1995:5). I agree with the anthropologist. To create categories when developing an understanding of certain micro-cultural groups is perhaps a necessary evil, but to leave these children in a category such as this denies them their individuality. This not only degrades them as children, but also steals from their uniqueness as individuals created in the image of God. Thus from this point on I will be using a term that more accurately describes the youth and children within our context. King David reminds us in his declaration of praise to God: *"For you created my inmost being; you knit me together in my mother's womb. I praise you because I am fearfully and wonderfully made; I know that full well"* (Psalms 139:13-14).

The uniqueness of each individual, of each child, must be retained, for if we loose this aspect, we lose what it means to be human. God created each hungry child that roams the streets in search of food. Our Lord *"knit"* them together with precision. To *"knit together"* implies a careful and deliberate action. For us simply to leave these children with "street children" as their anonymous given name would be unjust. I believe it is important to get to know the children with whom we work on an individual basis. I have visited feeding programs and soup kitchens where people simply become numbers. They no longer retain their individuality. Christ always took time to speak with individuals and to get to know them independently from the social program that was taking place.

I am certain that as Jesus and the disciples fed the five thousand on the green slope, there on the northeast shore of the Sea of Galilee, they took time to minister with individual people (see Mark 6:30-44). Other examples of Christ's ministry clearly show His interest in the individual person. One example is the woman *"who had been subject to bleeding for twelve years"* (Matt. 9:20a). Out of the crowd a desperate woman reaches out in hope of a healing. She touches the Messiah, the incarnate God Almighty.

How does Jesus respond to this woman? Does He look back only to see the crowd of faces? No, Jesus sees the person in pain. The Healer sees the wounded individual and ministers to her.

Another example is that of the leper found in Mark 1:40-45. Jesus expresses His compassion by bringing healing to one of the most outcast and despised of all peoples, the leper. Instead of being concerned about those who witnessed this act of mercy, Jesus reached out and brought healing to the individual created in the image of God. God's system of justice and dignity came crashing into this world's system of oppression. Jesus took time for this individual man who was hurting. Jesus' example of ministering to the individual in pain is an excellent example for us today. May we remember to look beyond the faces in the crowd and minister to the one who suffers.

The book of Jeremiah also reminds us of our uniqueness as humans, *"Before I formed you in the womb I knew you, before you were born I set you apart . . ."* (Jeremiah 1:5). The truth in this passage of Scripture is just as real today. Not only does the passage speak truth to our particular context of working with at-risk youth, but also it must overflow into every contact we have with our fellow humans. It is crucial that community children understand this important truth today. Almighty God knows each individual child. He knows them and *"knits"* them together in the womb. Scripture cannot be clearer in regards to this point of individuality.

"CHILDREN OF THE STREET"
... JUST ONE MORE HINDRANCE?

We are only adding to the hindrances these children encounter by continuing to use the term, "children of the street." Take Miguel for example. Miguel began his new life on the street at age twelve. I say his new life, because for him, it was new, at least for a while. Miguel grew up in a poor neighborhood in the city of Valencia, Venezuela. Miguel turned to the streets when his stepfather threatened his life one too many times. For Miguel, life on the streets was fun at first, no more threats from his stepfather and he could eat all the ice cream he could get his hands on. Over a period of time he got to know some of the young people on the street. They became his family, his community.

One day a Christian worker approached Miguel with a sandwich in hand. Miguel was now getting accustomed to handouts; he would even eat out of the garbage on occasion if the food looked appealing. The worker asked what life was like for a "child of the street?" At first Miguel thought the worker was referring to his friends, for he had never assumed he was at that level yet. Over the next couple of months Miguel continued to hear the term, "*niño de la calle*," from police officers and local restaurant owners. "Here comes that child of the street again," they would say. Miguel was used to being called different things, such as "loser" and "dummy," for this is what he often heard from his drunk mother, but now he was in a whole new level in society, for he knew what most people in the neighborhood thought of "*los niños de la calle*."

While the Christian worker in the story above certainly never intended it, he placed Miguel within a category that is most definitely looked down upon by the majority in Miguel's neighborhood. It is even possible that by calling children and youth, "children of the street," we are providing one more hindrance in their transformational process.

Children who are pushed onto the street are in a difficult situation. The obstacles are many. Why would we as Christian workers want possibly to place another obstacle in their way? The words we use to describe any child or adult must be thought through carefully. A common term for many homeless adults in the United States is the word "bum." I have heard numerous people use the term and have even heard pastors use it from the pulpit. What does this say to the world about us as Christians? If we consider these children as children who are "of the street," then they certainly must belong in the gutter. To use such a category is a misnomer of who these young people essentially are.

Some time ago a colleague of mine visited the former home of one of the boys we work with. As they approached the stairs to Marcos' home, Marcos refused to go any further. Instead of climbing the stairs, he looked down at his shoes, refusing to take another step. When the worker approached him to find out why he did not want to climb the stairs to see his mother, the boy said under his breath, "my mom doesn't want to see me." When the worker approached the home, to his shock, the mother yelled, "I always told him he wouldn't do anything with his life," as she glared at the boy. It is certainly true what Proverbs 18:21 tells us, *"The tongue has the power of life and death."* This was painfully accurate in Marcos' life, for he never lived to see his eighteenth birthday. One night as he slept an unknown assailant took his life.

As Christian workers, we must focus our words of affirmation on the child's uniqueness and proclaim the fact that these children are indeed *"fearfully and wonderfully made"* (Psalm 139:14). The fact is all children and young people need to hear words of affirmation. "Words of affection and endearment, words of praise and encouragement, words that give positive guidance all say, 'I care about you'" (Chapman and Campbell 1997:45). There is nothing more important than to communicate love and acceptance to children who have been abandoned. For many children living in at-risk circumstances, our words of encouragement might be the first positive words a child will ever hear. What we say about community children, whether in front of them or behind their backs, speaks volumes about our opinions of their existence.

I recently had the opportunity to share God's perception of children who live on the street to a number of boys locked up in a government detention facility in Venezuela. Víctor answered a question I had asked about whether or not they had ever heard anyone tell them that they were important. Víctor's answer was downright saddening. As I asked the question, "have you ever heard anybody tell you that you are important?" His response was "no, never." Several other boys followed up the question with, "No, I have never heard anybody tell me that." How sad! I then had the privilege of communicating God's love to them and to be the first person ever to have said "you are important."

I believe emphatically that we, the Church, must be

the ones that rise up with a prophetic voice and bless these children with words of praise and affirmation. The Father of the fatherless looks to us to be His voice in declaring these children as good. It is clear from Scripture that God declares them to be unique and created with a purpose. We must not waste any time. For now is the moment for action. Now is the moment to rise up and declare these children "precious in His sight."

What kind of image does the term "street kid" conjure up in the minds of the public? In South America, the term conjures up visions of rebellious youngsters and thieves. The term highlights the fact that these children are on the street and without a family. I believe God is asking us to go against these culturally sanctioned terms to find a better way of describing His creation. Perhaps we have coined the nomenclature from a point of unknown? Community children come to the majority of us with hands extended looking for a handout, or through a photo from a distant shore, but to those who work with these boys and girls day and night they have names like Michael, Monica, Christian, Fernando and Angie. Community children deserve a more accurate term.

COMMUNITY: AN ILLUSTRATION

An illustration from my Seminary days will help us understand why I have elected to use the more accurate label of "community children." While at Fuller School of Intercultural Studies, my wife Christina and I lived in an apartment complex with other students called the Cornerstone Community. We truly lived in a "global community." Many of our neighbors represented many nations. Along with their parents, many children lived in the complex as well. Children would often play off in the distance while I studied.

I can particularly remember one day quite clearly. There were about six little ones, ages two to seven, pounding and shaking the complex as they ran up and down the stairs, playing "hide and seek." As I studied I can remember the joy it brought me to hear the children laugh and giggle and to pound and stomp on the stairs. Laughter represents peace and joy, safety and comfort. The children were representative of many of our world's different ethnic groups. A few of the little girls were Korean, another little boy was Chinese and still others were Caucasian. The children played for most of the morning within the safe walls of the Cornerstone Community. Occasionally I would hear one child scream "help" or cry because of a skinned-up knee. My response was to jump to my feet to see if one of them needed help. I was not their parent, but they belonged to my community and they were under our protection at all times.

In this same way, the community from where these "street children" come, including the Church, must respond to their silent plea for help. Yes, perhaps my greatest reason for using this term is that it places responsibility back on society and the Church of God. When we use other labels that focus on the child's condition or situation, we do the child no good and we only escalate the belief that they belong on the streets.

A NEW WAY OF THINKING

My journey in working with at-risk youth has taught me much about the importance of life and dignity, especially life and dignity for homeless children. A shift in my thinking process has begun to occur since I first began working with these children. This change can be described as a paradigm shift, or rather a new way of looking at an old matter.

This process first began while I was working with the children directly, but it was certainly enhanced by a recent leave of absence for graduate studies. This new paradigm is devoted to the belief that families and society have abandoned these children. By calling them "street children" (my prior understanding) we are perpetuating the belief that they belong in the street for the word, "street" is their anonymous name. "If called a "*niño de la calle*" the individual appears to have the street as the most defining aspect of his existence. These terms disassociate young people on the streets from their families and communities" (Márquez 1995:6). If we are to say that the street is indeed the most basic facet of the child's livelihood, then we are no better than the person who placed the child there in the first place. Yes, someone has placed the child on the streets. It is my understanding that there is an injustice in stating that these kids belong in the street because they choose to be there. If this is the case, then we would be better off focusing our attention on other individuals who want to change. Those who believe that these children live on the street because they want to be there have never truly spent any time with them. There is a much larger issue at hand. It is my prayer that by using the term "community child" we will help bring about a change in the way many think about children who live on the street.

In using the word "community," I mean the very neighborhood and family from which these children have come. We cannot truly understand the children without understanding what kind of community they have come from. Whether the local church, a mission structure or a non-governmental organization (NGO) takes action, it must be done within the framework of the existing community, which includes the extended family of the child and his/her neighborhood. To work *with* the family to solve an issue is key. There is a big difference between telling the family how to solve an issue and working *with* a family to solve a matter.

Recently, while visiting a boy's family, I had the opportunity to interact with his mother about discipline issues. It seemed that every time Roberto would leave the house for a day or two he would return to severe punishment for having broken his mother's law. Roberto was often scared to return to his home, fearing his mother's reprisal. I wondered to myself if there was not a better way to help the family deal with the issue. Unfortunately I did not respect the mother's need to be part of the communication and thus the transformation never took place. Instead of telling the family how they should deal with particular issues, I should have led the family through a self-discovery process in our search for a solution. How many times do we as Christians approach particular issues with arrogance, thinking we have a solid Biblical answer, instead of allowing the Spirit of God to work in transforming the problem into a solution?

Josué and Héctor, as mentioned in the beginning of

this chapter, were rescued from the street at young ages. Both of the boys have gone through a radical transformation over the years. Like anyone who has gone through difficult events, scars remain, but restoration has taken place. This restoration occurred because some 'strangers' from the drug-rehab reached out to these boys and took them under their wings. The men that found the boys did not just say to themselves, 'there go some more street kids.' They took the situation seriously and recognized their responsibility to care for children in their community. Nowadays, both boys are walking with the Lord. Josué loves rapping about Jesus and going on mission trips. Héctor, who recently graduated from the program at the Lighthouse Ranch just got back from three months of living in a different country and attending a discipleship school for young people. Josué and Héctor are two young men that have progressed in their education and spiritual journeys. Good thing those men at the drug-rehab center did not just say, 'oh, there go those street children again.'

3

THE CHURCH'S ROLE

We have looked at the necessity of relating the street living child's predicament with the family and the community at large. Family and community participation is important, but there is another community that is crucial. The community that must be involved, in fact is vital in reaching these children, is the Church. I will refer to this particular group as "the Community" from this point forward. The responsibility to care for these children falls most heavily upon this group of people. In James 1:27 we are told *"Religion that God our Father accepts as pure and faultless is this: to look after orphans and widows in their distress and to keep oneself from being polluted by the world."* That is, if we call ourselves Christians we will care for those most outcast in our society, namely orphans and widows, especially in their pain.

Unquestionably, community children are in distress and calling out for help in the midst of their pain. Jennie Woods, President of Alliance for Children Everywhere, concurs with the importance of the Church's involvement in the lives of children at risk: "Children need professional interventions, but they also need meaningful relationships with ordinary people. They especially need the Christian community that is found within local church congregations" (Kilbourn and McDermid 1998: 263-264). Local congregations can minister to children that are homeless and abandoned.

Before we discuss how to receive such children into the Community, it will be imperative to discuss the concept of community, especially in light of Scripture.

The idea behind the word community in reference to the Church is central in our pursuit of understanding this issue. The New Testament clearly describes for us the importance of community in the book of Acts. The Church as the Community is a significant piece in understanding the new paradigm I am suggesting for our work with children and youth at risk. The Church in Jerusalem made a clear and counter-cultural statement as they stood in solidarity with one another. Acts 4:32-35 gives us several elements of what it means to live in the Community.

> All the believers were one in heart and mind. No one claimed that any of his possessions was his own, but they shared everything they had. With great power the apostles continued to testify to the resurrection of the Lord Jesus, and much grace was upon them all. There were no needy persons among them. For from time to time those who owned lands or houses sold them, brought the money from the sales and put it at the apostles' feet, and it was distributed to anyone as he had need.

As can be seen in this passage of Scripture, community life encompasses four crucial elements. If we are to have true community, we must have:

- Oneness in the Community
- Generosity in the Community
- Christ in the Community
- Equality in the Community

ONENESS IN THE COMMUNITY

We are told, *"All believers were one in heart and mind. No one claimed that any of his possessions was his own, but they shared everything they had"* (vs. 32). The people of God must be of one mind and heart. This oneness comes out of the Community's relationship with God. Is God in our midst? One must recognize the presence of the Almighty if one is truly to have oneness of heart and mind. I say that our oneness must come from fellowship with the Almighty because it is there, in the gathering around the King, where we find the King's rule. It is the King's rule and our common pursuit of His kingdom that unites us.

The apostle Paul splendidly asserts in unequivocal terms, *"Rejoice with those who rejoice; mourn with those who mourn. Live in harmony with one another. Do not be proud, but be willing to associate with people of low position. Do not be conceited"* (Romans 12:15-16). I like the way the Spanish version of the New International Version portrays the concept that the apostle Paul is trying to convey, *"háganse solidarios con los humildes."* To "be willing to associate with people of low position," is clarified by declaring that we are to live in *solidarity* with those of low economic and social status.

The idea here behind the word, *solidarity* is oneness. There is a sense of unity in the apostle's statement in this passage. To be one is to *"mourn with those who mourn."* Many of us enjoy rejoicing with others in their successes in life, but how many of us are so willing to mourn? Perhaps our ability to *"mourn with those who mourn"* is our true test of oneness? Oneness with those *"of low position"* is the Church's calling.

The apostle Paul reminds us why it is that many keep themselves from associating with people with less money, or of a different social status. The source is wrapped up in the word conceit. I once heard the famous protestant evangelist Billy Graham, in response to a question about homosexuality, say, "yes it is a sin, but the greater sin is pride." How right he was. It is pride that degrades and tears down others created in the image of God. It is certainly conceit that keeps us from reaching out to our fellow human in need. There is nothing like pride and conceit that can so destroy oneness among the Community.

In part, kingdom life involves following Jesus Christ as our Lord and copying Him! Like the popular bracelet: WWJD (What Would Jesus Do?). We can be certain that Jesus wants justice for all humanity including young men and women living on the street. As we minister, *"with one heart and one mind"* in bringing about God's way in the life of youth who live on our cities' streets, may we remember the fundamental teaching of Hebrews 13:3: *"Remember those in prison as if you yourselves were their fellow prisoners, and those who are mistreated as if you yourselves were suffering."*

There must be solidarity in our suffering with community children. There is no question whether or not they suffer neglect and abuse. There is no doubt that community children are mistreated. Scripture is clear with this point: If we are to live in harmony as the Community, we are to live in oneness with the most destitute in our midst, namely the hurting child. To walk hand in hand with those who suffer is to accompany them into the Community and to accompany them into the Community is ultimately to respond to our mandate of preaching the Good News of Jesus Christ to all.

GENEROSITY IN THE COMMUNITY

"No one claimed that any of his possessions was his own, but they shared everything they had" (vs. 32b). Many are surprised to find out that Scripture refers to material possessions more frequently than prayer and faith! Our heavenly Father is concerned about our material possessions! Why is it that after some two thousand years since our Lord came into this world there is such severe inequality and financial discrepancy between Christians around the world? Some have said, "this verse is simply a historical record, not an example for us today." Is that so? Why is it then that Scripture is so clear in its dealing with material possessions and equality in other parts of the Bible? As we will soon see, life in community has its costs. Unfortunately the western Community continues to be ensnared by its abundance while its neighbor to the south is indebted to poverty. The Church in the west must realize that the discrepancy is still too great. Ron Sider, in asking the question: "How generous are we?" makes use of some surprising statistical data. Sider reports the following in regards to giving in the U.S.:

- The average American citizen gives just 2.1 percent to charitable causes, according to the 1995 Statistical Abstract of the U.S.
- In 1992 church members gave 2.52 percent of their total income to their church (1997:204).

While the distinction between giving to the poor and the local church is certainly recognized, it must be understood that the majority of Christian giving is directed at the local church, thus creating a deficit in our responsibility toward the poorer brethren.

The Community is certainly hurting! No longer are we following the example given to us by the early believers. What has gone wrong? I believe the local church has lost its vision for giving.

Generosity within the Community of God must be a distinguishing mark. True community living will always include generosity with those most needy within the community. Self-denial is crucial to enabling generosity. Self-denial is saying no to our wants and yes to the needs of others. This was a part of the early Church's doctrine and should be present in the Community today. Abandoned children and homeless youth are vulnerable and should be cared for by the Church, within a context of wise, generous giving. The Church in the west must continue to partner with the worldwide Community of believers in our mandate of bringing hope to the hopeless child.

A clear biblical example of the Church acting out of a sense of responsibility can be found in 1 Corinthians 16:1-3. Paul, in writing to the Corinthians, asks that they "set aside a sum of money" as they are able for the poor in Jerusalem. This was a general collection for "God's people" because there was a need. There doesn't seem to be any hesitation on the part of these Christians. The giving of these responsible early Christians flowed from a healthy sense of solidarity with their fellow sisters and brothers. Paul asks that the Corinthians follow the example of others in the Community who gave generously, denying their own wants.

Some of the other examples include the Macedonian church in 2 Corinthians 8:1-5. Again Paul reminds the Corinthians of their abundance in using the Macedonian church as an example that they could follow. Paul says, *"For I testify that they gave as much as they were able and even beyond their ability."* What a solid example for the Church today! Generosity was a mark of the early Christian Community and it must be a clear and distinctive mark of God's people today.

To give generously to the Community's children means to give wisely. John Perkins, who has seen much damage in the inner cities of America from "acts of charity" warns us that charitable giving can be dangerous because donors frequently give without considering the damage they can cause. Creating dependence can be a dangerous charitable act (1993:23)! In both the Acts passage and that of Corinthians we are told that the acts of giving went beyond just "feel good" giving. The Macedonian church gave *"even beyond their ability."* There was sacrificial giving that went toward a real need. They gave without creating dependency and gave generously. Much damage has taken place simply because people have chosen to give in order to feel good.

I have witnessed first hand "acts of charity" toward children begging on the street. People often feel guilty when they see a child sleeping on the street or when they see a young person with their hand outstretched. Do the people feel good after they give change to a child? Yes, of course it cures any feelings of guilt, but the guilt-induced giving does nothing for the child. This is where we must educate those in the greater society and those in the Community that giving to alleviate guilt will not have a positive affect, but rather create dependency for the recipient and a false sense of hope for the giver.

One morning while meeting with some of my young friends on the street, I watched as one young boy collected money from businessmen and women as they walked to work. The boy received much that morning. At first thought, those who gave were really meeting a need, or so they thought. You see I know little David and have spent many hours talking with him about his drug problem. David is addicted to "piedra" (crack cocaine) and it will eventually kill him if he does not stop his use of it. Those who gave toward David's needs that morning were helping him in more ways than one. David has no problem finding food on the street, for he knows which store owners will give to him when he asks, but few drug pushers hand out their "candy" for free. Later that same day David handed over his new found cash and bought what no twelve year old, or anyone for that matter, should ever receive. In our generosity we must be wise.

CHRIST IN THE COMMUNITY

"With great power the apostles continued to testify to the resurrection of the Lord Jesus, and much grace was upon them all" (vs.33). An important aspect of the early Christian community was their passion for serving their Lord Jesus Christ. Not only were the early believers one in their unity

and generous with their possessions, but they also were vocal about their Lord. They freely declared that Jesus was Lord and that as Lord He rose from the dead to bring eternal life to all who might call upon His name. The Lord Jesus must take center stage in the local and international Community of believers. If He is not included, the Community will cease to exist in its primary goal of gathering the oppressed around the Healer.

There has been much discussion of the importance of the resurrection of our Lord for the Christian faith. This is not in dispute. I whole-heartedly accept and believe in the literal resurrection of our Lord Jesus from the dead. I endorse the importance of believing in the resurrection. As Donald Guthrie contends, the resurrection was the glue that held the early Believers together (1981:732). The resurrection should also hold us together today and our ministries to those on the periphery. Sure enough, there were others who followed the Messiah around awaiting His political move that would set Israel free from its Roman oppressor, yet it was those that were found still in the Community after His death, looking for the sign of His appearance, that created the divide between the faithful and the doubtful. The belief in the resurrection continues to be a divisive measuring stick today. Just as the resurrection was a standard in the early Community, so it must continue to be proclaimed in the Church of today.

The verbal endorsement of the death and resurrection of our Lord is needed today more than ever. Just as we are called to do good works so we are commanded to share the Good News of our Lord and Savior. Paul, in asking the question, *"And how can they hear without someone preaching to them?"* (Romans 10:15) implies our responsibility in sharing the Good News verbally with the world. If our ministry stops with our good works we are not truly involved with holistic ministry and we fail to fulfill our calling as the Community. The Community, as seen in Acts, proclaimed Jesus and Him crucified. Much has been said about the importance of evangelism and good works. Romans 5:8 declares authoritatively that Christ died for us because we are guilty of sin. The God of mercy died for us, *"while we were still sinners."* The Good News of Jesus is not complete until we have proclaimed the death and resurrection of the Savior.

How does the resurrection affect our ministry among marginalized children today? If Jesus had remained in the grave, hopelessness would have reigned. It is because of Jesus' resurrection that we have hope. Hope is a crucial ingredient for community children. It is because of the resurrection that we can minister in hope to those without hope. We can have confidence that God wants to apply the omnipotent power that raised Jesus from the dead to the lives of hurting people. The resurrection is a source of power for those in need. God has made a way for community children to be led into hope, having crushed the darkness and having provided the way. The resurrection of Christ from the dead makes all the difference in our ministry today, for if Christ had remained in that dark tomb, darkness would have prevailed. It is because of the resurrection that the Light of God has come into the world.

EQUALITY IN THE COMMUNITY

"There were no needy persons among them. For from time to time those who owned lands or houses sold them, brought the money from the sales and put it at the apostles' feet, and it was distributed to anyone as he had need" (vs.34).

To say that there was no *"needy persons among them"* is to declare that there was a sense of equality in the Community of God. This oneness was never forced upon anyone; it was simply a reality of the Community. It was a voluntary, spontaneous egalitarianism among the believers. The biblical account reminds us that the believers felt responsible to provide for those who were deprived of their basic rights (Guthrie 1981:735). The believers went beyond pity in the Community and allowed compassion to act out in the lives of those unjustly deprived of basic needs.

Active kingdom ethics in the Community should include economic koinonía as Ronald Sider (1997) describes it. Economic *koinonía* can simply be described as having a sense of fellowship in economic matters. Just as the early Church had interchurch sharing among the believers, if we are to model the given example, the Community must respond in kind. Lest we forget, believers in the United States are neighbors to millions of very poor children, Christian and not. When we look at the world scene, there is much disparity in economic koinonía within the Community.

Growing up in the United States in a wealthy suburb of Southern California has certainly made an impact on who I am today. I did not experience a shortage in the meeting of my most basic needs while growing up. Though my family did not always have what would be considered an abundance by North American terms, we certainly were never in want. My concerns as a young boy were caught up in having the most fashionable clothes and meeting the prettiest girls. I understand that some would argue I have no idea what it means to be a community child and certainly have no way of relating with them.

Despite not having grown up under a cardboard box, there were moments in my childhood when God's light and His call for economic koinonía came crashing into my soul. For instance, my father took me to visit an orphanage in Tijuana, Mexico when I was still quite young. God showed me through my experiences in that border city that there were indeed others in need. As I ran down the dirt road with some of my newfound friends I remember thinking, "why don't they have daddies and mommies" and "where are their shoes?" As a young boy it seemed odd to me for other children not to have dads and moms.

I am certain that experiences like this as a young person were used by my Lord to lead me into His work with community children. As I got older and continued to make trips into Mexico with my youth group from church, God continued to show me the disparity between the world I would visit for a week and the world I went home to. What was it that I was experiencing? I believe my Heavenly Father was showing me the sin in the inequality between His children. Why was it that some had so much while others so little, I thought. I now realize that there are certain structural issues that have helped us arrive where we currently are. Regardless of the "whys," we know that there continues to be a disproportionate sum of abundance in the west while the scarcity runs high in the south.

The abundance of which I was a part and in some ways continue to be associated with, has sharp contrasts with what I see on a daily basis. The shacks that litter my newfound city of Caracas are a constant reminder of my abundance. Each time I enter the home of one of the few boys that are still in contact with their families, I am once again awakened, as I was some twenty years ago on the dirt road outside of the orphanage. When I visit with brothers and sisters of the faith that live in the barrios of Caracas, I am jerked back into reality about the financial gap and the lack of economic *koinonía* that takes place today between fellow Christians.

Recently while living in Costa Rica I had the privilege of ministering alongside one of my *"Tico"* brothers in the small *pueblo* of San Miguel. As we visited with many of the local residents of this small rural town, I was impressed with the faith that flowed from these dear people. Many of them lacked the wealth I had grown up with, yet they overflowed in their abundance of love and faith. Yet, once again, the fruits of the economic *koinonía* that Scripture so clearly commands were absent from this local Community. By "fruit" I mean the results, the wise and generous giving from those with abundance, had clearly been neglected.

Economic *koinonía* is encouraged by Paul in 2 Corinthians 8:13-15 when he writes:

> *Our desire is not that others might be relieved while you are hard pressed, but that there might be equality. At the present time your plenty will supply what they need, so that in turn their plenty will supply what you need. Then there will be equality, as it is written: "He who gathered much did not have too much, and he who gathered little did not have too little."*

Paul seems to be drawing his reference from God's provision to the Israelites in the desert after they escaped their oppressors. In Exodus chapter 16 we see God providing for a desperate and hunger stricken people.

Somewhere between what Scripture describes as *"Elim and Sinai"* in the *"desert of Sin"* the people of God grumbled and complained to their leaders, Moses and Aaron. God in His mercy was prepared to *"rain down bread from heaven"* upon His children. The Lord provided for the Israelites through this manna as it is described (vs. 31).

> *The Israelites did as they were told; some gathered much, some little. And when they measured it by the omer, he who gathered much did not have too much, and he who gathered little did not have too little. Each one gathered as much as he needed (Exodus 16:17-18).*

To say that *"each one gathered as much as he needed"* implies that there were sufficient provisions for the people of God. It is probable that sharing took place between those more capable of collecting the manna and those who were sick or physically challenged.

The apostle Paul uses the passage found in Exodus to remind both the Corinthians and us today that there must be a sense of sharing and generosity within the community of God's people if we are really to be a community formed with kingdom values. We continue today to have those who are in need and destitute who must be led to the manna of God. The street living child must be considered part of our community. We, who have been given so much, have a responsibility to share with them who have gathered so little.

The Church is called to a global communal lifestyle, yet it has let its children remain outside of the walls. When we invite children on the street to join our family, our community, we are addressing the powers that oppress by declaring that these children are in our family and we are one with them. To oppress these boys and girls is to oppress the Community of God! It is clear that the world system is against their very survival.

One of God's purposes for our world today is that we recognize children living on the street as bearers of God's image, with dignity and rights. We are called to be partners in God's act of reconciliation. To reconcile children with their Heavenly Father is to fulfill God's desire that these children be protected and nurtured under the care of His Community. What will it take for this to happen? It will take the sharing of our resources with those that work with the community child. It will take working Christians to sacrifice and become one with these children who are in desperate need of help. Yes, it is possible to help meet the needs of community children around the world today.

THE STREET COMMUNITY

Where is the street living child's community? It should be with the Church, for we are their caretakers. But where is it actually? Many of the children on the street find their family in the forms of other boys and girls who are homeless. Throughout the world children look to each other for companionship and protection. The younger children often look to the older young people on the street for protection. This group and family activity has been well documented by Aptekar, Hecht and others.[10] Many of the boys with whom we have contact here in Caracas sleep together at night for protection. Who else is there to protect them? The street has become their community. It is clear from our perspective that this community can and often

10- See Street Children of Cali by Lewis Aptekar or At Home on the Street by Tobias Hecht.

does do more harm than good, but in the eyes and minds of the boys and girls, it is in the street community that they find protection. The street provides hope and liberty in comparison to their home situations. Our goal is to convince the children of a real hope and true liberty found in their legitimate Community of God.

The recognition of the street community is crucial if we are to reach out to these children. This group has become their substitute family for the time being and thus we must accept this reality. To ignore this family is to underestimate the power of a sense of community. I have been using the term "community children" instead of the more commonly used category, "street children" because I believe it is important to reach these children within the context of their community. What is in the street community that creates a sense of security for them? What kind of felt needs is the street community meeting? These are important questions we must consider if we are going to reach these children effectively and give them an opportunity to better their lives. We will soon look more closely at some of the answers to these questions. As we actualize the values of the kingdom of God in the city, in reaching homeless children and adolescents, we do so with community at the very heart of our message. Jesus, by dying on the cross, provided entrance into the kingdom to all who will come. True kingdom work is done in community, fashioned in the likeness of Christ and His proclamation of reconciliation and hope.

THE ROLE OF THE LOCAL COMMUNITY

Many local churches around the world have a sincere desire to reach out in the love of Christ to children at risk but they often do not know where to begin or how to go about it. Part of our ministry to community children includes mobilizing the Community as a whole to support the ministry to these and other children at risk. Why do I feel that this is so important? Because I believe with all of my heart that ultimately the responsibility to care for homeless children lies with the Church. Over the years, ministry for me has included the mobilization of local churches to participate in outreach among community children. The following story is one example of how God used a local representation of His Church to start the healing process for one family at risk.

Some years ago Jorge walked up to me as others and I were preparing to leave for the beach with a group of children. Jorge asked if he could come as well. This was our first time connecting with this boy, but we agreed to let him join us. Back in the early days of ministry, we would often pack the children and teenagers into a van, with surfboards on top and go to the beach. I am quite certain we were the only outreach team in Caracas, perhaps the world, which would take homeless boys and girls to the beach for surfing, but the kids loved it and so did we. It was in moments like those that we were able to connect with the children and really develop solid relationships. Jorge had a blast at the beach that day! Upon returning to the city, we began looking into his circumstances.

After some research, we found out why Jorge was living on the street. Like many community children, Jorge was mistreated by his stepfather and was asked to leave the home on a regular basis. We went through the legal process and invited Jorge to live at the Lighthouse Ranch. After several months of living with his new family, Jorge made a decision to follow Christ and to be baptized. Jorge was baptized in a little Baptist church that had been partnering with the ministry from the very beginning. On that day, two boys from the home, Jorge and Ivan were both baptized. Over the months that Jorge was living at the ranch home, we were also able to meet with his mother and stepfather. Our desire was to see Jorge reinserted into his home. One major obstacle, among many, we faced with that family was the practice of *"Santeria"* in the home.

Santeria is a form of witchcraft practiced in Venezuela and other parts of Latin America. It was not uncommon to see the family lighting candles and praying before the gods they had on their altar. On the Sunday of his baptism, Jorge's mother, Rosanna, came to watch. At the end of the service she gave her life to Christ. To see Jorge's mother receive Christ was joyous. God began his work in the family using that little church.

It is immensely joyful for the Lord to use local congregations to bless community children and their families, not to mention the joy and encouragement it brings to the members of the local church. There are many churches around the world participating in the effort to reach homeless children and other children at risk and for this, God will certainly bless their efforts. Unfortunately there are, as well, churches that are more concerned with their building programs, music entertainment and cushioned pews than placing the child in their midst and blessing him or her. Is this not what Amos depicts when he cries out:

> *I hate, I despise your religious feasts; I cannot stand your assemblies. Even though you bring me burnt offerings and grain offerings, I will not accept them. Though you bring me choice fellowship offerings, I will have no regard for them.*

Away with the noise of your songs! I will not listen to the music of your harps. But let justice roll on like a river, right-eousness like a never-failing stream (Amos 5:21-24)!

Justice includes setting free the street dwelling child. Justice includes actively defending those who have been trampled upon. Rather than worry about temporal church paraphernalia we are exhorted to heed the call of Jeremiah:

"Cry out in the night, as the watches of the night begin; pour out [our] hearts like water in the presence of the Lord. Lift up [our] hands to him for the lives of [our] children, who faint from hunger at the head of every street" (Lamentations 2:19).

As Christian ministers to the community child, in addition to our responsibilities in carrying for the hurting child, we must also fill the role of prophet in our church-es. New Testament prophets were not terribly concerned with foreseeing the future, rather they were used by God to exhort the Church to follow the path of God. That is our role today! But whether we are exhorting God's people, or ministering to a child in need, we must be determined to love, with an unconditional love, with the love of Christ. 1 Corinthians 13, the love passage, admonishes us to love, even when we do not feel like it and the Apostle Paul reminds us, *"If I give all I possess to the poor and surrender my body to the flames, but have not love, I gain nothing"* (vs. 3). Without a doubt, the children we minister to will *"gain nothing"* as well, if we are not consumed by the love of God. So whether it be encouraging the local community of believers or talking with a desperate child, may we love, as Christ loves.

4

STRATEGIC COMMUNICATION

Upon arriving at Simón Bolívar International Airport in 1995, just outside of Caracas, I can distinctly remember feeling the warm humid air hit my face as I walked outside of the terminal for the first time. Everything was exciting; a new home and country, new faces and a new language. Very soon that initial excitement turned into frustration and confusion. Venezuela was where I believed God had called me to minister, yet I could tell immediately that I was not in California and that I had much to learn before I would begin to have the ability to do what I had gone there to do, minister to community children. Learning to speak with the children in Spanish was difficult, but I eventually got to the point where I was able to communicate. It was at this point, where I could speak the language, that some of the frustration disappeared. Soon enough I learned that working with community children and other at-risk youth meant I needed to learn a new language (street lingo) and a new culture. The youth and children that I had begun to get to know had been on the streets for years and had literally developed a microculture (subculture) that was quite different from the mainstream Venezuelan culture.

In our work with these children at risk, we have sought to understand what it means to be homeless in this mega-city. Yet we realize that we will never understand what it means to have to survive on these mean city streets. We have learned that to manipulate is an unfortunate necessity for these children and youth and is recognized as a survival technique. As has been mentioned, these children form a microculture and similar cultural traits can be found throughout the world in bands of homeless and at-risk youth. In order to understand a microculture, we must first understand the concept of culture. Culture can be described as "learned and shared attitudes, values, and ways of behaving" (Grunlan & Mayers 1988:39). Thus a microculture will also include these factors of the larger culture with details unique to its own system. What and how this micro-system looks like will depend upon the makeup of the group and its larger cultural leanings.

Now that we have come to some understanding of culture, it is also important to define the concept of "microculture." As Carley Dodd explains, a microculture "refers to one or a combination of (1) groups we choose to associate with, (2) collective identities we prefer to maintain, (3) demographics we may represent, and/or (4) ethnic and family origins we may experience based on birth" (1998:61).

Perhaps my social-cultural group as an adolescent will bring some light to this issue. At age eleven I learned a new sport, surfing. I actually found an old broken surf-board in the trash and took it home for some repairs. After my father and I put the thing together, I gave it a shot. I tried surfing. At first surfing was just a sport, but as time went by I began to associate with other "surfers." Eventually the inside pressure (and advertising) began to affect my speech, dress, body language and attitude. In much the same way, a child on the street will receive in-group pressure to act, talk and behave in certain ways according to the group's certain collective identity. Typically among community children and youth one will see certain social identity and loyalty. Many micro-cultural groupings of these children have much in common. A quick survey suggests the following items in common:

- Common Adversaries
- Common Empathizers
- Victimization Concepts
- Common Codes and Speech Patterns (Dodd 1998:66)

In order to communicate contextually with community children, it is crucial we understand that these children function in such groups.

In this chapter I intend to consider the plight of home-less children and a number of effective ways in which we can communicate with them, ultimately with the goal of reaching them with the Gospel of Jesus Christ. In order to reach community children, one must be able to communicate effectively with them on their turf and within their world. We will look at a number of communicational strategies not only from my personal reflection but also through a number of cultural anthropological sources.

THE AUDIENCE

One important aspect of intercultural communication is getting to know your audience. We must intentionally choose a group that we wish to help (Kraft 1991:144). Jesus chose a particular group to communicate with. This is clearly seen in Matthew 15:21-28. While Jesus was in the region of Tyre and Sidon a woman came to him seeking relief for her daughter who was possessed by an evil spirit. Jesus replies *"I was sent only to the lost sheep of Israel."* The woman, a Greek, replied to Jesus by telling him that she wanted just the *"crumbs."* Jesus goes on to heal her daughter because of her faith, showing that we, too, must have compassion and be careful not to neglect those who are not in our intended audience. While Jesus did not neglect the woman, He still held to his primary focus. This is the balance we ought to aim for as well in ministering to one segment of society. Clearly Jesus' primary audience while on earth was the *"lost sheep of Israel."* Christ even segmented His audience more when He reveals that He did not come for the healthy ones, but only for the sick sheep (Matthew 9:12).

While in Seminary, I lived in an Hispanic community in Los Angeles, California. I was overwhelmed with the needs of the people in our community. To whom was I to minister? How was I to do it? After some prayer, God showed me that I was to get involved in teaching and helping lead a group of teenage boys who were struggling with gang involvement. Many of the boys had either been involved in gangs or were tempted to do so. With so many needs around me, I could easily have involved myself in ten different ministries, yet God directed me toward one group within the larger society. Who is your audience? To whom is it that God has called you to minister? As has been mentioned earlier, we must show care in not "batch processing" the children we come into contact with on the streets. Placing drug addicts in a home with children who have spent a couple of months on the street or who only work on the street is unwise. Let's be careful to distinguish whom we target in our ministries.

ON THE STREET: PAST EXPERIENCES

As I think through this topic on strategic communication, I am reminded of many instances when I have been working with children on the street, thinking that I was communicating effectively with them when in fact I was not. One example of this is how easily many of the boys and girls would say the "sinner's prayer," that is, pray to receive Christ into their hearts. Perhaps they were sincere, yet I still feel that others and ourselves did not effectively communicate what praying to receive Christ meant. Did the youth on the street see it only as a way to gain our attention? Even worse, as a means to manipulate us into thinking they had changed their lives? Ultimately, their sincerity in whether they received Christ or not is in the hands of God, yet I still wonder if there is not a better way to communicate the need they have for Christ and His forgiveness.

We often meet with the children and youth early in the morning. Our purpose in going at this time is that we know they are usually either just waking up or are still sleeping. If we miss them, they are often much more diffi-

cult to locate and are probably roaming the city somewhere, so it is crucial that we catch them before they
awaken and are gone. During these contact times we usually go out in groups of three or four after some prayer
time as a group. In the past, volunteers have often come
dressed up, looking as if they planned to go to the theater
afterwards. I often wondered how this made the youth
feel. Did the way the others or I dress put an even larger
gap between us and the boys and girls on the street? The
community children usually wear their clothes for days
and even weeks at a time. This is a critical point. We must
be careful in what we wear to meet them on the streets,
realizing we are not living on the street, yet we do have a
responsibility, in my opinion, to lessen the gap between
the youth and us.

Another example of what could be interpreted as ineffective communication can be seen in our sincere desire to
meet the physical needs of the children on the streets. God
loves these children and desires to see them leave the
street, yet we are called to meet their physical needs (i.e.
food, clothing and housing), while they are still on the
street. Often we met these needs by reaching out to them
on the street and by supplying them with clean clothes
and food. Our intention was to communicate with them
by meeting their needs and showing that God loves them.
My question is, is it possible that the community children
interpreted our gifts differently from our original inten-
tions? Is it possible that we were helping them to sustain
their lifestyles on the street? I still believe in providing for
their most basic needs, yet we must do so with care and
wisdom.

One more example of ineffective communication is

something I see on a daily basis. As has already been mentioned, often I see children and youth with whom we work, sitting in the subway stations begging for money. People walking by will often give them money, thinking that the children are going to use it to buy food or clothing when in fact they go directly to the drug dealers. I believe people are very sincere at times and desire to communicate their interest in the lives of these children, yet they are in fact telling the kids "if you live on the streets, people will give you money for free." This is perhaps one of the most destructive messages a child on the street can hear! What they need to hear (especially those new to the streets) is about the reality of street life and its consequences. What if all the people who gave the children money stopped doing so and started giving money to them indirectly through a non-profit organization working with such young people? What a blessing it would be, ultimately, for the children if people would stop feeding their drug habits and begin helping to provide solutions.

CHRIST, THE SUPREME COMMUNICATOR

Kraft in his book, *Communication Theory for Christian Witness*, deals with the most important aspect in Christian intercultural communication, that is, our relationship with God. We must start with Christ, for He was and is the greatest communicator ever to have walked the planet. Christ came with the message that God forgives and desires reconciliation between Himself and humankind. Christ "carefully established and maintained the kind of intimate relationship with God the Father that humans are meant to live" (Kraft 1991:5). Christ is our supreme example. If He had an intimate relationship with God the Father, how much more do we need this kind of a relationship with God? Jesus' dependence on the Father was the key in His communication to His audience. In John 5:19 Jesus says *"the Son can do nothing on his own; he does only what he sees his Father doing."* Jesus was not saying that He didn't have the power to do anything on His own, for He surely did have this power. He was God in the flesh. But rather He willingly followed the will of His Father. In Philippians 2:6-7 we are told that Christ *"Who, being in nature God, did not consider equality with God something to be grasped, but made himself nothing, taking the very nature of a servant, being made in human likeness."* It is in this "nothingness" that Christ was such a powerful communicator. Jesus willingly gave up His right to use His power and, in perfect fellowship with the Spirit of God, He sought to do that which the Father wanted Him to do. Just as Christ was dependent upon the Father, if we are to be effective in our communication to community children and teenagers, we must be dependent upon God as well.

INCARNATIONAL COMMUNICATION

Jesus' incarnation itself is a powerful example of effective communication. In John 1:14a we are told, *"The Word [Jesus] became flesh and made his dwelling among us."* This verse tells us that God became a human being, like you and me. God chose to communicate with us by becoming one of us, yet not ceasing to be God. The incarnation is perhaps the greatest and clearest communication from

God to humankind that we can see. Just as the incarnation is God's communicational strategy, so should it be ours if we seek to follow God and become effective communicators. It is important to note that Jesus came as an infant and had to learn the ways and culture of the people He was to serve. I can remember learning Spanish and how foolish I felt when I could not pronounce a word. I felt like a child, I was not able to communicate all that I desired to communicate. I usually had to point or use my own form of sign language to get the point across. So Christ, too, had to go through this period of learning.

Perhaps the greatest example of Christ's incarnation was His servant-like heart. Jesus tells us in Scripture that if we desire to be great (and effective), we must be a servant. In Mark 9:35 He says, *"If anyone wants to be first, he must be very last, and the servant of all."* Perhaps this is one of the reasons He was so effective in what He came to accomplish on the earth. Not only did Christ speak the message to us, He lived it through the incarnation. If we are to have an impact on community children and youth, we, too, must live the message of the liberating Gospel!

The implication of the incarnation for us as communicators is that we, too, must learn from the people to whom we are called to minister. It is crucial that the children on the street be our teachers, and that we allow them to be our guides in learning all that we can about their lives and microculture. When we become learners, servants and living messages, we will then be in a better position to communicate the love of God with these children.

COMMUNICATING IN STREET TIME

In dealing with community children one must recognize that they run on a different clock than most of us. One way we go about evaluating their sincerity in wanting to leave the streets is to set up certain times to meet and talk with them. As a North American I am quite aware of being on time, but I soon found out that the youth on the street see time quite differently. None of the boys have watches, and some perhaps do not even know how to tell time. I have often spent at least an hour, if not more, waiting for the boys at the designated waiting area.

Carley Dodd in his book, *Dynamics of Intercultural Communication*, deals with different concepts of time. Dodd says, "Our understanding of time falls under a class of nonverbal communication called chronemics and is influenced by culture" (1998:146). One's concept of time is powerfully influenced by culture. Within every culture of the world one can assume a different perspective on time. For some it is extremely important to be punctual while for others being an hour late is okay. These different concepts of time will influence our communication behavior. For example, since living in Latin America I have experienced a different concept of time from that to which I am accustomed in the United States.

In dealing with time, Dodd refers to two ways of understanding it. Most cultures fall into these two categories. They are *polychronic* and *monochronic* time categories. One example of this is seen in a comparison between the U.S. and Latin America. The United States typically falls in the monochronic time category while Latin America tends to lean towards the polychronic category. Dodd says, "North Americans tend to think of time as a road or long ribbon stretched out in a progressive linear path, having a beginning and an end" (1998:146). Americans see time as important, thus the phrase "time is money." Time can be spent, wasted and bought, while most Latin Americans see time as more flexible, with the priority being people and relationships, *not* time.

In working with these unique children we must remember that they have a much different concept of time than even their larger cultural grouping has. Time is certainly not important to them, for they have no reason to follow a clock. When they are hungry they find something to eat; when it is time to take a nap they simply find a place on the ground and doze off. Tobias Hecht in his study of community children in Northeast Brazil mentions the fact that it was often difficult for boys and girls to respond to questions about time.

> The questions that referred to time were difficult for the respondents. For instance, the question asked of the children in shelters, 'How long have you been here?' was regularly answered with such replies as um bocado de tempo, meaning loosely, 'a bunch of time' (Hecht 1998:5).

Hecht goes on to explain that they would often try to overcome this problem (the kids' lack of understanding in regards to time) by asking them if they remembered what soap operas were showing when they left home (soap operas in some parts of Latin America are seasonal) or by asking the children about certain festivals or holidays to find out approximately when they left home and arrived at the shelter.

In communicating to these children and adolescents, we need to meet them on their turf and in their world. There is nothing inherently wrong with not having a watch and not knowing what time it is, thus, we should first adapt to their sense of time. Once the children are under our care, it will be important to teach them to adapt to their culture's concept of time. One way for us as street educators to overcome different perceptions of time would consist of looking at events or certain seasons of the year to deal with the youth's sense of time. One possible way to meet youth during the middle of the day (12 noon) would be to tell them to meet when people are out for lunch. At noon people are walking the streets and eating lunch. Regardless of our tactics in communicating, we must remember to adapt to the children's sense of time.

COMMUNICATING PERSON TO PERSON

One of my primary roles in the past, outside of direct work with the youth, was in public and church relations. That task took me to a variety of churches, encouraging people to become involved with our ministry through financial support and volunteer work. Many people responded to our request for volunteers and full-time workers by saying they had no experience in working with community children or felt inadequate. They felt as though they would not be able to relate to the kids and their lives on the street. I myself have felt this at times. Growing up in middle-class North America in no way prepared me to work with these boys and girls, yet I believe that in many ways God has provided a way for us to relate to them on a personal level, a human level. We can and are able to relate to them as humans, as people who have emotions and who need to be loved just like anyone else. Yes, I agree that there is wisdom in having "ex-street children" reach out to those still on the street but I do not believe that this is the only way. God has called people with different types of backgrounds to minister to homeless youth. This is what makes cross-cultural ministry so important. Why has God called so many people to minister across cultures? God has placed within us, as human beings, the interest and curiosity to learn from and listen to people from other cultures. I have much more interest in listening to a lecturer from another culture, with his or her own biases, than I do listening to someone from my own culture. There is something about the diversity of culture that intrigues us as humans. This is one of the reasons why I believe in cross-cultural work among street youth living or dwelling.

Often, the status or class of the street educators and child-care workers varies from that of the children. In the case of community children, many who work with them are not only from a different class but also from a totally different lifestyle and culture. The best possible type of relationship we can have is one where a human communicator fully realizes that he or she is simply trying to communicate with another human (Kraft 1991:151). What often happens is that we see the people we are trying to "convert" or minister to, not as other fellow human beings but rather what Kraft (borrowing from Loewen) calls a "station to station" relationship (1991:151). A "station to station" relationship is based on position and status, not on a personal level. As Christians, we must move towards the understanding of "person to person" communication and reject the "station to station" relationships as not Christ-like.

One way in which we can move from a status level to a personal level is through our intentional ability to fully identify with those we are communicating with (Kraft 1991:152). By identifying, I am not suggesting that we go and sleep on the street, although some have done this, but rather that we find areas of common interests. As Christian child-care workers, we must not only learn what it means to be Venezuelan, Colombian, Kenyan etc., but also a child on the street. We will never fully comprehend what it means to be a child who was born impoverished, abandoned and abused on a regular basis, not to mention living on the street, but we can attempt to put ourselves in their place in order to empathize with them.

One day I went downtown and forgot to bring enough money to get home on the bus, so I decided I was going to look on the ground until I found enough money to get home. I did my best to conjure up the strength to beg, but in the end I conceded to my pride and took a taxi, which I paid for when I arrived home. I did get a small glimpse, however, of what it must be like to be on the street and not have any money. Dallas Willard, in his book, *The Spirit of the Disciplines*, gives a number of great examples on how to relate to the poor. Willard suggests shopping where the poor shop and taking public transportation with the poor (1988:213). Perhaps a midnight snack with a homeless child, on the side of the road or a week without a shower would help one to understand a little more what it is like to be a community child.

Instead of always focusing on the differences I believe

it is also important to find areas of commonality. This must be initiated on behalf of the communicator. I do not believe for one second that kids on the street are worried about our not being able to relate with them. They do not sit up at night worrying about our inability to understand where they are coming from. Rather they greet us in the morning usually with a smile (but sometimes a demand for food), realizing that we might be the only people in the world they can trust, that is if we have indeed earned their trust. Some common areas we have of interest with the youth are: 1) appetites 2) desire for fun 3) the need for families 4) the need for emotional support (friendship) and 5) the need for God. These are just a few of the areas where we can find commonality with the children and adolescents. What is most important, though, is that we relate to them as humans communicating to humans. We, as intercultural ministers, are not above them. We must make this clear to the children we reach out to.

Henri Nouwen has a number of profound points to make on this subject. Nouwen left his prestigious academic position at Harvard University and moved into the L'Arche community where he lived with and ministered to the mentally handicapped. Nouwen knows what it means to relate and minister to the *"least of these."* He did not put himself above the people he worked with. He found himself on their level, a human relating to a human, created in the image of God. In his book, *In the Name of Jesus*, chapter three is called, "From Leading to Being Led" and it deals with a number of crucial issues if we are to minister and communicate as Christ did. Nouwen says this in regards to what he was learning in the L'Arche community:

I discover that I am learning many new things, not just
about pains and struggles of wounded people, but also
about their unique gifts and graces. They teach me about
joy and peace, love and care and prayer—what I could
have never learned in any academy (1989:57).

I believe that as we reach out and try to communicate
the love of God we must do it as a learner, taking the low
position, and not that of someone who has it all together,
with all the answers. If we are to relate and communicate
to community youth and children we must not fall for the
temptation to be great and popular. We must minister
with the love and humility of Christ.

COMMUNICATING WITH OPINION LEADERS

It is important that we get to know who the opinion leaders are in each group (gangs in many circumstances). Most
of the youth on the street in Caracas have someone they
look up to in their group, yet when it comes to survival it's
everyone for him or herself.

Most children and youth who live on the street choose
to be in groups and there is usually one who is respected
by the others. This is also true with Burundi community
children. They "move in groups, each with a leader."[11]

Peer groups are nothing new; they have existed for
centuries and serve a purpose. Those children who find
themselves on the street are no different than any other

11- All Africa Press Service, February 9, 1998.

social group. They desire to be with others that have similar interests. While peer groups exist in almost all cultures, the purposes behind them vary. Community children, for example, find security in their group. Often children will sleep together in order to keep warm and safe.

These groups of community children are crucial to our understanding of their microculture. In each group there tends to be opinion leaders, those to whom the rest of the group adheres. There are usually ten to fifteen children in each group. One group was labeled the Gómez/Gomita group, after two brothers who had spent many years on the street. Seemingly, the youth that have been on the street the longest are those that receive the most respect (Márquez 1995:10). One problem here, for those that desire to minister, is that the youth who have been on the street the longest are the hardest to persuade and usually have a strong dependence on drugs. In Colombia, those that lead the group of community children are referred to as *'jefes'* (literally, bosses). Again, those that lead tend to be older and are respected for their "size, strength, athletic ability, intelligence and street sense" (Felsman 1982:63).

Once these opinion leaders are reached it is thought that others will follow. Opinion leaders are people who are respected and followed. Their opinions and beliefs carry more weight (Kraft 1991:154). Opinion leadership is often informal. It is finding those that have influence and know what is going on. They are simply those with more power and sometimes more wisdom than others. This is a crucial point if we are going to be able to communicate the goodness of Jesus Christ effectively.

Some time ago we were blessed to see one of these

opinion leaders come to Christ and leave the street. God did a tremendous work in the life of Douglas while under our care at the ministry's Lighthouse Ranch. One night a few of us from the ministry went to the funeral of one of the boys from the street. At the funeral home we ran into about a dozen of the kids from the street. Douglas came with us that night; I must admit I was a little apprehensive about bringing him because I knew his old friends would be there. God did something powerful that night! Douglas began to talk with the other boys about their need for Christ and the importance of leaving the street. The boys listened to him that night, much more than they had ever listened to one of us. I believe one reason for this (other than the Holy Spirit's action) was that Douglas was an opinion leader. He was looked up to by the other youth (See chapter 7, A Movement of God, for more on how God is using Douglas today).

While ministering to pre-gang members in Los Angeles, California, we had a regular group of teenagers who met with us on Wednesday nights in our home. Within the group of eight regulars who would show up, there was a definite opinion leader. Carlos had the respect of the group and as leaders we knew we needed to get Carlos on our side if we wanted to get anywhere with the other members. Getting the opinion leader on your side can make the difference between having a cooperative response or a chaotic one. I am *not* saying that we must wait for the opinion leader to come to Christ first before we reach out to the other children on the street. We need to be loving toward all as Christ would, especially to those that have recently arrived on the street, and persistently encouraging them to leave; but at the same time we must continue to persuade those older leaders to forsake their street environment.

FELT NEEDS AND DEEP-LEVEL NEEDS

It does not take long for one to realize that children living on the street have a number of very real needs. Most of the young men and women on the streets have substance abuse problems and are often involved with crime in order to get their "fix." This life of crime puts many children in a very dangerous place. It is obvious to those of us outside of their realm that they have tremendous amount of needs, yet the enemy has blinded these kids into thinking that they do not need a home and a family. The adversary has told them all they need is their freedom and drugs. Ultimately these children need Jesus Christ and His love! But what are some of their other needs? What are their physical needs? What are their emotional needs?

I refer to these important needs as their "deep-level needs" (see Kraft 1991). Deep-level needs are needs that often go beyond people's capability to articulate. While these deep-level needs are crucial, many times the children do not recognize these needs. Because they do not always recognize their deep-level needs, often we must start with their felt needs. We need to ask ourselves the question, what do they sense are their needs? We must put ourselves in their shoes, or within our context, their lack of shoes, and ask ourselves, "if I were a homeless child, what would my felt needs be?" Christian child-care workers should try to understand what the crucial felt needs of the children are (Kraft 1991:68-69). We know that community children's deep-level needs are family support, unconditional love, a home, nutritional food, education, and a relationship with Jesus Christ. But what do *they* believe are their needs?

One obvious felt need and deep-level need is food. Providing food can be an important link in getting to know community children, especially at first. We as an organization have a policy against giving the children money. It is definitely important to remember that giving them money will only create more difficult problems in the future, so providing for their needs, even while on the street, can be done through food provisions.

Another way to meet their felt needs is through curing their wounds. I cannot tell you how many kids I have bandaged up on the streets of this city. In making contacts with the youth we carry around a very basic first-aid kit. For the most part we clean up superficial wounds but every once in a while, we are confronted with bullet wounds to the legs or something just as bad. I have noticed throughout the years that cleaning their wounds puts a trust between them and our team members. If they can trust us to clean their wounds, how much more can they trust us in other areas of their lives?

Community children have a felt need for having fun. These misnamed "street kids" are *children* and love to have fun. In the past, once a week we would meet them at a particular spot and take them to the beach or the mountains for the day. They absolutely loved this and would continuously ask us if we could go out again to the park or beach. One way that we can possibly use this desire for fun is to communicate to them how much fun it can be to live with a family. It is also important to have activity days at the home with those children who have chosen to leave the street. Using fun activities as a reward can be a positive way to encourage them to leave the street.

Freedom is also a felt need that many community children have. Many of the boys and girls continue on the streets and refuse to leave because they feel they will lose their freedom. Often the children say they left home because there was no freedom. Obviously we need to keep this in mind when communicating with them. Certainly we can use this need for freedom to share God's love with them as well as the freedom He brings to us through setting us free from the chains and strongholds of the adversary.

People often respond in shock when they find out that community children have fears. I myself first thought that they did not have fears, but in reality they do. Children sleep together at night because they fear what people will do to them while they sleep. Many are afraid of spirits and demons and what can happen to them if they are attacked. Security, or release from fear, seems to be a very real felt need. Here is what one child says about his fear, "Sometimes when I'm on the street I live in fear. I only get a little high because if you get really high you mess up, you fall to the ground, and then someone can come along and kill you . . ." (Hecht 1998:40). Community children have every right to be afraid, for many have been killed on the street. Nancy Leigh Tierney documents a number of murders on the streets of Guatemala involving community children (1997:246). In 1992 while on a short-term trip to Bogotá, Colombia, I was told of accounts of homeless children and youth being drugged and after they had fallen asleep, their kidneys and/or other organs were taken to sell on the black market. I cannot say whether this was true or not, yet the reality is, the children were afraid. One boy in Colombia always made sure he had a knife under his bed at night. I was constantly trying to tell him that he was safe in the house, yet he still lived in fear.

What are some ways we as Christian street educators can help community children in regards to this felt need? One way we can help is to show them the power of God. We believe God is always present and watching over them and us.

He is their Father who wants to protect them. It is also crucial that we confirm the safety of the home that we provide for them. While the youth do not feel as though they need a house to sleep in, perhaps showing them that their safety will be guaranteed will help meet some of those felt needs. While many of the youth need inner healing and counseling for a number of their fears, I feel that by meeting their initial felt needs we can move them closer to a place where we will have access to address their deep-level needs. It is important first to acknowledge their felt needs before going on to their deep-level needs. By meeting these initial felt needs we can find a bridge in which to help them where they are, fearful and full of pain from the emotional scars that are left over from years of severe abuse and neglect. Ultimately meeting the felt needs of the children and youth is our entrance into being able to dig deeper and put the children in touch with the true Healer. Meeting felt needs will lead us to helping provide for deep-level needs (Kraft 1991:69).

FATALISM

Another key factor to be aware of is fatalism. Fatalism is the belief that one is not in control. The locus of control is in the hands of the gods. The belief that one lacks the power or ability to change their condition can be problematic for the child-care worker. However, for a homeless child addicted to cocaine paste, who has been told he or she is worthless since age five, humanly speaking one does not see much hope. What must be communicated is the power of God! For Christian child-care workers, our hope is based on the omnipotence of God and the fact that the Lord is deeply empathetic towards the community child's needs. It is crucial that we understand the microculture's perspective on this if we are to be effective cross-cultural and micro-cultural communicators and build upon the stepping stones provided for us in our work.

INDIVIDUALISM VS. COLLECTIVISM

There is value in recognizing the validity of cross-cultural communication theory in our work among community children. Not only is this theory important for the cross-cultural worker, but for the "cross-microcultural" worker as well. Dodd outlines some important differences in individualist and collectivist cultures. In our ministry to children, we must take the time to understand the cultural tendency, and of course, the subculture. Our effectiveness will depend on it.

Individualist perspective:

- Concerns personal achievement
- Concern for clarity, directness
- Truth telling and straight talk
- The meeting of personal needs and goals rather than group needs and goals
- Self-referent messages, more "I" than "we"
- More independent
- Linear pattern of conversation

Collectivists emphasize:

- Community, groupness, harmony and maintaining face
- Indirect communication
- Concern for others' feelings, avoiding embarrassing situations
- Avoiding negative evaluations from a listener
- Less goal direction
- More interdependent, group concerned
- Fewer linear patterns of conversation (1998:92-93)

Generally speaking, collectivist cultures tend to be Asian, African and Latin American whereas the individualistic cultures tend to be North American and European.

Understanding the host culture's perspective is key if we are to reach the microculture efficiently. It is important to come to an understanding of the group of children we are working with. Observational research will prove helpful in coming to a conclusion on the collectivity or individuality of the children to whom we minister.

In conclusion, we have seen the importance of learning both cultural patterns and microcultural understandings when relating to children in cross-cultural and microcultural contexts. God is at work, calling people from different nations to work with community children across the world. I believe God wants to continue to raise up a body of concerned believers in bringing hope to these children, but we must do so in the understanding that the cultural lenses we look through are certainly different coming from a little homeless child.

5

THE KINGDOM OF GOD AND ITS CHILDREN

A PAINFUL REALITY

A sad fact today is that many of our churches preach their church and not the kingdom of God. Is there a difference you ask? The answer of course is YES. There is a tremendous difference, and our response to this question will create a difference in how we minister. Are we seeking simply to grow our church or are we seeking to extend the kingdom of God? To grow a church is not necessarily wrong when done for the right motives, but to neglect the extension of the kingdom because of an over focused effort on growing one's church is misguided.

In the following pages, the kingdom of God will be a theme that we focus on. What does the kingdom of God look like to a homeless little girl? How does it affect a young man living under a bridge? How do we explain the kingdom to a mistreated boy living in a poor squatter area?

As we continue in our pursuit of understanding community children, we do so with the understanding that we are most definitely not living under the full rule as the following studies will show us.

In research done by Covenant House on the streets of New York City, the seriousness of the street life was brought to light:

> Out of 150 street children interviewed, 41% reported abusing alcohol and/or drugs, 59% met the criterion for a diagnosis of conduct disorder, 49% had a major mood disorder, 52% reported a manic episode (a period of very high energy and feelings of euphoric well-being), 37% reported chronic clinical depression and 32% met the criterion for post-traumatic stress disorder. Forty-one percent said they had considered suicide and 27% had attempted it, some more than once. Further, street youth that were beaten, sexually molested or had a child were more likely to attempt suicide (Kilbourn 1997:61-62).

Truly, many youth on the street around the world have been similarly treated. A study in 1991 in Guatemala by the Center of Orientation, Diagnosis, and Treatment of Sexually Transmitted Diseases and Casa Alianza examines the context in this part of the world:

> 100% of children interviewed had been sexually abused, of whom 53% were abused by family members; 5.95% were abused by friends; 2.7% by neighbors; and 46% by people they didn't know.

With issues like these it is no wonder children seek out a safer place to live. Community children have many urgent needs that should be met when seeking to provide intervention. As we will soon see, the rule of God will and is, changing the values of this world. The very values that have done so much harm in the lives of these children will be brought to light and transformed under the coming rule of God.

Community children need the whole Gospel. Many Christian NGO's and churches in the past have only focused on leading children to Christ. As many different churches and groups have experienced around the world, it is not uncommon for the children to go up front for an "altar call" every time it is offered. Kraybill notes there is often a "false split between spiritual and social" issues within the Christian Church (1990:29). This "split" leads people into ministering only with the children's spiritual or physical needs in mind. Instead of splitting the two, thus dividing the Gospel, we ought to see them as both/and. While ministering in Caracas we have come across organizations and people who would only "convert" or "evangelize" the children, while other groups would only meet the physical needs of the youth by providing them clothes and education. Both of these are crucial if we are to minister effectively among street living youth. Evangelism and social action are inseparable in ministry to at-risk youth!

We must realize that there is no single way of reaching community children with effective intervention. There are many ways that need to be included if we are to have an impact. The children on the street are whole people and as whole people they have physical, emotional and spiritual needs. In ministry to community children we must include this holistic approach. If we seek to extend the kingdom of God, it will be important to focus on the whole child.

In the following paragraphs I would like to highlight God's concern for community children by presenting His heart for them as seen in Scripture. These verses need our attention if we are to mobilize the Church to reach out to homeless youth on the streets. In the following passages we will notice a crucial area that must be dealt with if we are to have a solid theological basis for reaching community children in a holistic manner. This area touches upon the theological aspect of the kingdom of God and how it relates to children on the street.

THE LIFE OF A COMMUNITY CHILD

A few years ago I was in a small cafe, drinking a cup of delicious Venezuelan coffee and eating an *arepa* (a corn flour patty, filled with a variety of choices) when a young boy on the street approached me asking for some money. This was not the first time this happened, in fact it occurs quite often. I invited the boy to sit down next to me (which the waiters did not appreciate very much) and shared my *arepa* with him. He was extremely sleepy, almost falling asleep at the table, but he managed to tell me his name and age. "My name is Calvin," he said, "and I'm twelve years old." This was the first time I had seen Calvin on the street, but from his appearance he seemed to have been there for a while. His clothes were torn and dirt had begun to collect on his arms and legs, almost looking as though he had rubbed them in thick grease. I was surprised to hear that he knew where his mother lived and visited her quite regularly. After a few minutes Calvin said *"adios"* and headed back to his familiar stomping grounds on the street.

It was a year and six months later when I ran into Calvin again. He was again close to the restaurant where I first met him. He was just as dirty and neglected as the first time I saw him. This time was different from the first time, though; he seemed to show some interest in talking with me. From that point on I have seen Calvin off and on, always by himself and usually very happy to see me. On one occasion while I was making contact with the youth, a co-worker accompanied me as I contacted the children on the street. When we came across Calvin, my co-worker asked him why he trusted me. His response made an impact on me as he said, "because, he is my friend." Calvin was the only kid that I can remember calling me his friend. This caused a great deal of concern for him within me. This concern I have for Calvin is from God, for surely the concern God has for Calvin is profound.

THE ADVOCACY OF GOD

The Father is ardently concerned for youth that take to the street to escape abuse and oppression at home. Therefore, where God speaks of the oppressed and the poor, how much more must the Lord be concerned with the poorest of the poor and the smallest and most vulnerable of the oppressed? Scripture speaks clearly and succinctly about God's concern for the poor, oppressed, fatherless, orphaned, afflicted and about children in general. Homeless children are all of these, thus God's concern for community children is found throughout Scripture.

Children living on the street are fatherless. Psalm 10:14 says, *"But you, O God, do see trouble and grief; you consider it and take it in hand. The victim commits himself to you; you are the helper of the fatherless."* God is concerned, He considers their situation and He understands their dilemma. His desire is to help and nourish the fatherless. God is constantly watching over the fatherless and protecting them. Psalm 10:18 states that God is in the process of *"defending the fatherless . . . "* The Father's heart aches for those children that have no one to protect them. Perhaps one of the most destructive elements that has led to children living on the street is the lack of involved fathers.

Many children living and working on the street are orphaned and fatherless. In Exodus 22:22 God clearly states that He will pour out His wrath on those that in any way hurt or *"take advantage of a widow or an orphan."*

Community children are the oppressed. This oppression often comes in the form of abuse by police and other authority figures. We are told that God *"upholds the cause of the oppressed and gives food to the hungry"* (Psalm 146:7). The God of the Bible does not forget what happens to children on the street. A key verse in dealing with the oppressed and fatherless says this:

> The Lord is King forever and ever; the nations will perish from his land. You hear, O Lord, the desire of the afflicted; you encourage them, and you listen to their cry, defending the fatherless and the oppressed, in order that man, who is of the earth, may terrify no more (Psalm 10:16-18).

This passage is wrestling with the concept of theodicy. Throughout the Psalms we see this issue over and over again. I too have had to think through this subject in regards to the homeless child. To be honest with this Psalm we must understand the context. The context that is being discussed here deals with wicked people in Israel's society and their prosperity in the midst of the righteous who are poor and oppressed. While this passage was speaking to a specific issue at the time of its writing, it prophetically deals with the issue at hand. For we know, *"The Lord is King forever and ever . . . "* (vs.16). The Lord is King! King of what? The Lord is King of His kingdom, His people, and His children. The King's law was revealed to the Israelites in Exodus 22:22-24. It is here that we are told, *"Do not take advantage of a widow or an orphan."* If these people are taken advantage of, the Lord's *"anger will be aroused"* (vs.24a). God is the Father of the orphan and will act swiftly and justly in response to his or her oppression.

In Psalm 10:18 we are told that God will defend *"the fatherless and oppressed, in order that man, who is of the earth, may terrify no more."* Homeless children truly know what it means to be terrified by humankind. Numerous children around the world have been brutally killed and abused. In ministry I have come across children as young as eleven who have been shot by the police. The children will on occasion steal food or other things and be shot in the leg as they run away. God says there is coming a day when He will judge those who have hurt and terrified children. And on this day the unrighteous and unjust will be judged by the King of all authority.

A New Testament passage also deals with God and His concern for those who harm children. Jesus says, *"But if anyone causes one of these little ones who believe in me to sin, it would be better for him to have a large millstone hung around his neck and to be drowned in the depths of the sea"* (Matthew

18:6). God's advocacy is long reaching and effective. His resolve is great and mighty.

In Caracas there are many drug dealers who keep the boys and girls on the street busy pushing drugs. There are also everyday citizens, who give money to the kids just to get rid of them, unaware that the kids will go off and smoke that money in the form of 'crack' cocaine or marijuana. There are those who oppress the kids by buying them drugs if they rob and steal for them. A good friend and co-worker witnessed one of the boys on the street breaking into a car, stealing the stereo and then passing it off to a vender who in exchange for the stereo handed him a can of shoe glue. Many community children will do anything to get what they need. Shoe glue is an addictive drug that the children inhale to get high. Psalm 72:4 says that God will *"crush the oppressor."* God, the advocate of community children, will judge with complete justice those who oppress children.

Community children are the poorest of the poor! The children with whom I work in Caracas are consistently in need of nutritious meals, baths and clothing. Their only resource for food is primarily through begging or stealing.

Psalm 35:10 tells us that God will, *". . . rescue the poor from those too strong for them, the poor and needy from those who rob them."* Our Lord is concerned about the poor. Throughout the Scriptures God mentions the poor and His heart for them; God is their shield and defender. Homeless children are the poorest of the poor and should be in the Church's focus!

Community children are afflicted! Homeless children have been afflicted in more than just one way. They have been afflicted with every type of social rejection and atrocity. Job, in referring to God, says that he *"gives the afflicted their rights"* (Job 36:6). God watches over street dwelling children youth and desires to meet their needs by giving them that which they deserve, that which has been withheld from them, life itself. Children deserve to have food, a home, family, education, love, and the opportunity to love others and the support of the society. Community children have none of these rights. God declares that He will provide them with rights.

Community children are indeed children. We are encouraged by God to rescue innocent children in God's love. In Proverbs 24:11, God calls upon us to be active in rescuing the innocent with much persuasion; *"rescue those being led away to death; hold back those staggering towards the slaughter."* This is the Community's responsibility. We are to be the instruments of God's compassion and mercy in the world, including the extension of God's kingdom among abandoned children. Proverbs 24 goes on to say, *"If you say, but we knew nothing about this, does not he who weighs the heart perceive it? Does not he who guards your life know it? Will he not repay each person according to what he has done"* (vs.12)? The Lord certainly does not hold back in holding His people accountable for those that have been sinned against.

Clearly God is calling upon us to "stand in the gap" for those who are oppressed. As we can see, God is concerned about individual homeless children. I take comfort in the fact that God is working and moving on behalf of street dwelling children all over the world.

THE REIGN OF GOD OVER HIS CHILDREN

As we have already seen, community children are important to God, regardless of society's indifference and outward negligence. While God certainly does not endorse things such as stealing, robbing and drug addiction, He is most definitely concerned about homeless children and adolescents, regardless of their present actions. Throughout the New Testament Christ is seen mixing with "sinners." In many cases the Pharisees looked down upon Him because He spent too much time with them. In Luke 7:34 the Pharisees are recorded calling Jesus a *"friend of tax collectors and 'sinners.'"*

While deviant behavior must be addressed through street outreach, intervention programs and values education, we are still called to follow the example of Christ and to *"preach the good news to the poor . . . proclaim freedom for the prisoners and recovery of sight to the blind, to release the oppressed, [and] to proclaim the year of the Lord's favor"* (Luke 4:18-19). This passage is central to the kingdom of God paradigm presented in the record of Christ's ministry on earth. We should be compelled, just as Christ was, to *"release the oppressed"* and to *"preach the good news to the poor."* Community children are poor, oppressed and in need of God's forgiveness, release and healing.

The kingdom of God is a much-debated issue. Theologians have argued and debated the term and have confused this important topic for centuries. One thing is true; Christ places the kingdom of God at the center point of His ministry.

Ron Sider agrees that the kingdom of God played a central role in the ministry of Christ (1993:51). In whatever we do, including work with street dwelling children, we must place the kingdom of God at the heart of our ministry and message.

What exactly is the kingdom of God? Throughout the Gospels we see Christ referring to the kingdom as both a current and future phenomenon. Much of the debate among theologians about this rule of God centers on the issue of whether or not it is a present or future reality. One of the most comprehensive and understandable books dealing with this issue is George Eldon Ladd's, *The Gospel of the Kingdom*. An important point that Ladd makes is that the Church is not the kingdom, but rather it is God's instrument in extending the kingdom. There is no doubt that God is using His people, the Church, to bring extension to the kingdom. Ladd states that the kingdom is God's "kingship, his rule, his authority" (1959:21). God's authority is at work in our lives and in society as we, the Church, extend the work of God through social kingdom work and the preaching of salvation. The good news of Jesus is that He came to forgive humankind of sin; this is crucial in our understanding of this paradigm. The kingdom is primarily the reign of God as King in our lives. God cannot be King in our lives without the reconciliation that Jesus came to provide through His death on the cross and His resurrection from the grave. The coming of Christ as Messiah was the initiation of the kingdom of God on earth. Jesus boldly declared freedom and release to those oppressed by sin and Satan and his values on earth.

Many believe that the kingdom of God is only a future reality, while others see it as only a present truth. Ladd believes that it includes both a present and future realm. Sider notes, "There is a growing consensus, however, that Jesus viewed the kingdom as both present and future" (1993:55). Today, we see parts of God's kingdom active in our world. Similar to rays of light breaking through on a cloudy day, so the kingdom of God is seen when it breaks through the present world with God's values. When a street dwelling girl who is involved in prostitution, as some are, is rescued from the street by a church or Christian ministry, so we see God's kingdom breaking through evil with good. When a person is handicapped from birth and then is healed, we see kingdom values shining through. In no way do we see the full reality of God's kingdom today; however, we do see certain aspects of it. While I do not believe the kingdom will be fully extended by the Church, I do believe that God is definitely using His people to permeate the world with His kingdom principles. Ultimately it will take Christ and His coming to establish the fullness of the kingdom of God (Ladd 1959:24).

In Kraybill's book he investigates two kingdoms, one is the kingdom of this world and the other is the kingdom of God. In reference to God's kingdom being upside-down he says, "The Gospels portray the kingdom of God as inverted or upside down in comparison with both ancient Palestinian and modern ways" (1990:19). It is important to note that Kraybill in no way endorses people abandoning this world and building a Christian empire, but rather we are to live in the world under God's present kingdom rule. The important emphasis is that we put into practice kingdom values while we are still in this world.

In this upside-down kingdom we see those who are mighty and prestigious brought down low and those who are considered outcast and lowly, lifted up high. Community children, in this upside down kingdom are on top. In this view of the kingdom, down is up and up is down. The Body of Christ is to be the instrument that raises up homeless youth through a holistic ministry to stand before the world and show them as valuable and worthy of respect. Through this mighty act of God, the raising up of these children, the Lord will transform society by turning the world upside down.

COMMUNITY CHILDREN AND THE KINGDOM

God loves children! In the Old Testament God is seen primarily as their protector, while in the New Testament we see God's love expressed through Jesus' reaching out to children and blessing them. Christ shows us his concern for children all over the world as we see Him placing His hands on them and blessing them in the Gospel of Mark 10:13-16. The story goes like this:

> *People were bringing little children to Jesus to have him touch them, but the disciples rebuked them. When Jesus saw this, he was indignant. He said to them, "Let the little children come to me, and do not hinder them, for the kingdom of God belongs to such as these. I tell you the truth, anyone who will not receive the kingdom of God like a little child will never enter it." And he took the children in his arms, put his hands on them and blessed them.*

"People were bringing little children to Jesus to have him touch them" (vs.13). The children spoken about here were probably from the age of toddlers to pre-teen. The Greek word (*paidia*) is used by Mark to describe the children. This is the same word used in the passage regarding the twelve-year-old daughter of Jairus in Mark 5:35. Regardless of the age of the children, Christ was quite interested in them and their well-being. It was not uncommon during this time for Jewish rabbis to lay their hands on children and bless them. The parents were doing what

any normal Jewish parent would do. The question we have to ask is, why would the disciples *"rebuke them?"*

It's not stated why the disciples prevented the children from coming to Him. Maybe they felt it would be an inconvenience to Jesus; they obviously didn't see this ministry as very important. Even today children are often overlooked in Christian literature and within mission organizations. Fortunately things are beginning to change. There are, in fact, some organizations and literature beginning to focus on them, though in our world today, there are many who don't see ministry to children as all that important.

Anyone who has worked with children can most likely sympathize with the disciples' frustration over this apparent distraction. One needs an incredible amount of patience in working with children, especially those children who are at risk and in crisis. In my work with children and youth in Venezuela, a child in need of help or a listening ear has on occasion called me in the middle of the night.

On one particular night in Caracas I had just settled down to watch some television when the phone rang. When I answered it, someone on the other end asked, "do you know Christian?" I responded by saying "Christian who?" The man went on, "well, Christian is in jail and he needs some food!" After figuring out who Christian was I told the guy that I would be there the next day. I had no interest in going that night. The last thing I wanted to do was go to a jail somewhere downtown. Immediately he asked, "Are you Gregorio with *Niños de la Luz* ministries?" Kind of embarrassed I said, "yes I am." Harshly he told me, "There is a kid here named Christian, he's hungry, now are you coming or not?" Christian was a boy I had been in touch with from the street. I had given him my business card with my telephone number on it in case he ever needed to call. He was 14 years old and homeless when I met him and now I had to make the decision of whether or not I would respond to my promise of helping him. I think because of the man's harshness I decided to go. It turned out that Christian had been in jail for two days without food.

I can remember entering the little police station. I met the man who called who turned out to be a police officer at the station. Christian had been picked up for not having his identification card on him. I can remember looking in the dark cell and seeing Christian packed in there with 10 adult prisoners. I gave him the food I had bought and then sat down with the commander of the station. He began asking me questions while he was cleaning the bullets from his revolver with a paper towel. Talk about intimidation! Once the officer found out who we were and that Christian was a minor, he let him out that night. What was originally an inconvenience and interruption to my night turned out to be a total blessing in disguise, especially for Christian, and it taught me an invaluable lesson.

In this passage, Mark goes on to tell us that Jesus became righteously angry with the disciples: *"When Jesus saw this he was indignant"* (vs.14). Jesus' anger is understandable. Just a few days before:

> *He took a little child and had him stand among them. Taking him in his arms, he said to them, "Whoever welcomes one of these little children in my name welcomes me, and whoever welcomes me does not welcome me but the one who sent me"* (Mark 9:36-37).

The disciples had probably just heard Jesus say this

and here they were preventing the very ones Jesus was talking about from coming to Him. It should be noted that this is the only time in Scripture when we are told that Jesus became *"indignant."* This clearly portrays the priority that Jesus wants to give children in the world.

Surely Jesus must be indignant about the state of the world's children today where malnutrition and poverty affect their lives with incalculable pain and suffering. Here are just a few heartbreaking realities:

- Malnutrition and starvation kill some 34,000 children under the age of 5 daily (Bread for the World, 1996).
- By 2003, 15 million children under the age of 18 had been orphaned by HIV/AIDS. (State of the World's Children, 2005 Report: UNICEF).
- At least 250 million children between ages 5 and 14 must work for a living in developing countries (Report: Beyond Child Labor, UNICEF).
- An estimated 800,000 girls in Thailand between the ages of 12-16 are involved in prostitution (UNICEF).
- 300,000 young people under 18 are exploited as child soldiers (UN Office of the Special Representative for Children and Armed Conflict: 2003)

In the midst of so many horrendous situations with community children at their center, God is at work in His kingdom, and He is using the Community to extend it powerfully. Patrick McDonald, says in an interview conducted by *Pulse* (a missionary news bulletin) that there are 110,000 full-time workers and 20,000 ministries working with children worldwide. He goes on to say, there are some 2 million children at risk being cared for in evangelical ministries (Guthrie 1997:2). God's kingdom is being extended today, yet there is still much to do.

Community children belong in the kingdom. When the Church prays, *"your kingdom come, your will be done on earth as it is in heaven,"* we are praying that God's kingdom (and its values) would take effect now in the lives of street dwelling children and others living in desperate situations.

"He took the children in his arms, put his hands on them and blessed them" (vs.16). Jesus' righteous indignation did not stop at the emotional level, but rather He turned this deep sense of pity into action. Our response to information about children living on the street must also turn into action. Our *pity* will be transformed into *compassion* by putting action to our emotion. Jesus put His hands on these young children and He touched them and thus blessed the children. By touching children with a blessing we are extending God's kingdom on earth as it is in heaven. Christ truly is concerned with children! Jesus is the greatest child's advocate!

Jesus has set the example! He placed kingdom values into His ministry among adults and children. Now it is up to us, His Church, to minister in a like way. May we remember to see street dwelling youth and children through the eyes of the Father of the fatherless and remember His desire to extend His kingdom on earth as it is in heaven, where:

> *The wolf will live with the lamb, the leopard will lie down with the goat, the calf and the lion and the yearling together; and a* **little child** *will lead them. The cow will feed with the bear, their young will lie down together, and the lion will eat straw like the ox. The* **infant** *will play near the hole of the cobra, and* **the young child** *put his hand into the viper's nest. They will*

neither harm nor destroy on all my holy mountain, for the earth will be full of the knowledge of the Lord as the waters cover the sea" (Isaiah 11:6-9) [emphasis mine].

6

PRINCIPALITIES AND POWERS

The Church is "a community that lives and demonstrates the liberating power of the gospel and the new possibilities available in Christ for a world oppressed and enslaved by demonic principalities and powers" (Costas 1974:53).

What are these new possibilities that Costas speaks of? Certainly the liberating power of the Gospel includes freedom from the enslavement of personal sin. Could it also be in reference to freedom from structural sin? We will soon see that Scripture indeed refers to oppressive structural sin and its influence over the destitute. Yes, the Good News certainly does enslave us to righteousness: *"and having been freed from sin, you became slaves of righteousness"* (NASB Romans 6:18). But does this also include freedom from oppressive systems? We will soon see whether or not this is true.

One day while working at the ministry's Lighthouse Ranch for children, we received a phone call from a young girl named Ana. Ana had called to tell us that she was ready to leave the streets of Caracas and join us at the home. Those of us who worked at the Lighthouse were excited to receive her, for we knew that life on the street was killing her. Four hours later she was seen walking down the dirt path to the home. We were delighted about this decision she had made, yet were clear minded about the tremendous sacrifice it would take for her to remain. It was not unlike her to change her mind about leaving the street. Almost six months prior to this day she had spent a week at the Lighthouse Ranch and decided she preferred the streets.

The first couple of hours were smooth and Ana seemed to be fitting in with the other children just fine. Some time toward mid-afternoon something happened. Ana became quiet and withdrawn. When we approached her to find out what the problem was she ignored us, turning her face away. After a while one of our female volunteers pulled her aside to see if there was anything we could do to help her with adjusting to her new environment. It was at this time that she told us that she wanted to go back to the street. Some five hours after first arriving at the ranch she was now ready to return to the street. By this point Ana was crying and cursing at us to let her go back to the street. Each time I prayed for her she yelled louder. At one point while we were talking with her she broke a window with her hand, which she apparently did not even feel. Eventually Ana got to the point where we were no longer able to hold her in the home. We let her go back to the street. The next time I saw her on the street she was addicted to "crack" cocaine, dirty and malnourished.

What would cause a young girl to refuse our love and

want to live on the street where she must fight for her life on a daily basis? Why do other children on the street reject our invitation to leave their precarious environments and live in a safe place? I believe the answer to these questions can be found in Scripture. *"For our struggle is not against flesh and blood, but against the rulers, against the authorities, against the powers of this dark world and against the spiritual forces of evil in the heavenly realms"* (Ephesians 6:12). The very root of the problem is a spiritual conflict that is taking place and keeping children, such as Ana, on the street and in spiritual chains. There is a struggle occurring right now over children like Ana. This struggle is going on all over the world, within thousands, if not millions of youth and children who desire to leave their concrete beds and drug diets for a safe place. In our work with community children we have talked with numerous boys and girls on the street who truly desired to leave, yet there was something or *someone* who prohibited them from doing so. We are told that, *"our struggle is not against flesh and blood."* Getting children off the street is not a matter of being elegant in our persuasion tactics, nor is it our strategies as much as it is relying upon the power of God. It is important to have strategies when working with community children, yet we must not allow these strategies to take priority over our reliance upon the power of the Holy Spirit who has come to convince those who are of this world of their sin (John 16:8). One important thing that we must realize is that there are spiritual strongholds that are keeping these children in captivity to their ways on the street.

PERSONAL STRONGHOLDS

Peter Wagner has been a big proponent of spiritual warfare and warfare prayer. While I personally have some concerns about some concepts he is promoting, I do believe his input will be helpful in the following pages. He believes that spiritual strongholds must be defeated before our evangelism and social action will see any results (1992:65). The issue of strongholds is an important one and we must address it if we are to have any success in our ministries to at-risk youth.

The terminology, 'stronghold(s)' is used quite often in Scripture. j116

2 Corinthians 10:4,5 tells us, *"The weapons we fight with are not the weapons of the world. On the contrary, they have divine power to demolish strongholds."* A stronghold is an area (person or structure) where the enemy has taken over and become the boss. A stronghold is not easily released. In the lives of the children, we know that the enemy and his forces are finding areas where they can strike at children and keep them in despair. George Otis, Jr. defines strongholds as "nothing less than satanic command and control centers" (1991:129). Demons seem to search for areas where they can take control of a person's life. While this is not the place to discuss a theology of demonization,[12] it is safe to say that Scripture endorses the fact that demons do and can influence human beings (i.e. Matt. 8:31; Mark 1:34; 6:13; Luke 8:38; 1 Tim. 4:1 etc.).

12- See the following works for further study into this area: Naming the Powers by Walter Wink and Engaging the Enemy by C. Peter Wagner, et. al; Dark Angels by C Peter Wagner & F. Douglas Pennoyer.

Community children and youth have experienced much abuse. Marcela Raffaelli has found abuse to be all too common in her research of why children take to living in the street. In her article, "Family Situation of Street Youth in Latin America," Raffaelli refers to the following study: Fifty-five percent of one sample group in Colombia (Harrison, in *Asociación Salud con Prevención*, 1987) and forty percent of the sample from Brazil (Hutz et. al., 1995) made mention of the fact that they had left home because of violence (1997:89).

Perhaps one of the reasons Satan is able to take such powerful strongholds in the lives of these children is that of harbored anger. In my experience in working with youth living on the street, I have discovered that many of them struggle with anger and bitterness. Due to some of the horrible trauma and abuse that these children have suffered, forgiveness is an important issue. Ephesians 4:26, 27 says, *"'In your anger do not sin'. . . . and do not give the devil a foothold."* These children and youth need to be led into areas of forgiveness and healing from the abuse that they have received from family members and others. It is not until they are able to forgive their abusers that some of the footholds will be released and thus Satan will have nothing to accuse them with (see Revelation 12:10).

Dan Brewster of Compassion International agrees that abuse is connected with the spirituality of the individual child. Brewster in writing about sexual abuse says, "Sexual abuse strikes at the core of the individual. The two deepest forms of intimacy are sexual intimacy and spiritual intimacy. Violation of sexual intimacy has implications for our spirituality" (Kilbourn 1998:147). As ministers we are called to assist children and youth in their healing. Phyllis Kilbourn and Marjorie McDermaid have edited a book that can assist us in our effort to bring healing to the lives of sexually abused children and youth.

We are advised in Scripture that *"the devil prowls around like a roaring lion looking for someone to devour"* (1 Peter 5:8). Satan is seeking to devour children around the world. Certainly the enemy uses sexual abuse as his tool to destroy these young lives (Kilbourn 1998:147). Unfortunately this is a widespread problem and includes many more children than just those that are homeless. God is raising up His Church to get involved in rescuing and healing the lives of children who are being sexually exploited and abused in our world today. The Viva Network has recently launched a project called the ASHA forum, which is seeking to gain a standing in this world to protect and heal such children.

SYSTEMIC STRONGHOLDS

While I do not believe that social structures can be demonized as a person can be, I do believe, along with Wagner and others, that demons can actually influence, if not control, social and political structures. Certainly, our very own fallen nature, greed, power and corruption aid the demonic in setting up unjust systems and structures.

I believe this issue is important for all of us, including children on the street, who find ourselves living within social structures. In the same way that Satan will gain a stronghold on a person, so he seeks to gain strongholds on nations and institutions. Walter Wink and Robert Linthicum have completed some important research in regard to this issue. Although Wink and Linthicum come from different theological viewpoints on this issue, they will prove helpful for me to lean upon as I seek to understand how this issue affects community children.

GOVERNMENTAL STRUCTURES

I first began talking to Daniel about leaving the streets on a rainy day when I found him tucked away in a dry little corner. He was asleep as usual so I had to awaken him with a delicious pastry; the smell seemed always to do the job. Soon Daniel was up, a little bewildered, but he was awake. As both of us now took up this little dry corner, out of the rain, I began to talk to him about his dreams and desires. This soon led into a discussion about leaving the streets and going to the boys' home.

We already had a couple of boys there who were growing and beginning that transformation from children of the street to children of Light. Daniel surprised me and said that he would like to get off the streets and begin to learn how to read and write and to change his life. After talking a little more we decided on a place where we could meet the next day in order to take him to the ranch. Soon it was decided upon and I left thanking God that finally Daniel's time had come. After seeing him now for two years on the street, finally he was making this important decision!

The next day I met up with Daniel and a friend of his, Luis. It seemed that Luis wanted to leave the streets, too, and begin his new life at the ranch. Wow, I thought, praise God! I had arranged a ride for the boys through a co-worker. Now we just needed to get to the arranged meeting place. It is not always easy to travel through the city with homeless kids. Many bus drivers will not even let the kids on the busses and the subway refuses to allow them into the station, yet somehow we managed to get there. Soon enough we were at the location waiting for my co-worker to pick us up. The hour we had arranged for the pick up came and went making it even more difficult to wait with these two anxious young guys. As I sat there watching for our ride (by this time the two had fallen asleep), I noticed two police officers walking our way, fast, as if something serious were taking place. When they arrived where we were, they yelled at the boys to wake up. One of the kids, half asleep, made the comment, "What, are you going to kill us?" The officer immediately slapped Daniel hard, leaving me astonished, wondering where he found the right to do this. Fortunately the kids left and hid around the corner as I tried to explain what I was doing with them and how they had been just about to leave the street for a boys' home, before they (the police) arrived on the scene. This situation is not uncommon. While we must show wisdom, I believe we must confront these "powers" with the truth of God's word.

Governments have responded to the massive number of youth living on the streets by locking them up in detention centers around the world. It is not uncommon for the authorities to either push kids back into their *barrios* (shantytowns) or to lock them up in closed institutions that totally deprive them of their basic human rights (Márquez 1995:210). Some years ago the National Institute for the Welfare of the Minor (INAM) sought to eliminate the problem of homeless youth in Caracas by placing them into their detention centers. They believed the only way to rehabilitate these children was to place them behind bars and barbed wire and force them into a drug rehabilitation program. The program did not succeed and the children are once again on the street.

Márquez has carefully documented these coercion tactics that are used against community children (1995:136). If we are truly to have an impact on bringing freedom to these children, it will not come by forceful intervention. The children themselves must come to their own conclusion that they need help. Jackson Felsman in his dissertation gives detail to some historical approaches of force intervention. In 1968 during the Pope's visit to Bogotá, Colombia, for the Eucharistic congress, the children were put away and "swept" up. Many Colombian citizens became concerned about the children and began to inquire into their whereabouts. Felsman also listed some more current "street sweeps." A number of children on the streets began to disappear due to the need for clearing the "eyesores" in Cali, Colombia (1982:71-72).

What is the difference between coercion and voluntary removal? Voluntary removal is when permission to be taken from the street is granted by the child, and all necessary laws are adhered to. Following all legal requirements is crucial. The following definition shows us that coercion goes against the basic rights of the child:

> **Coercion** involves using force or threats to compel or constrain a person to act in a manner contrary to that person's free will choice. Force applied may be physical, perhaps using weapons. Or it may be the psychological pressure of fear, using threats against a person's freedom, property, family or life. Usually the oppressor will

claim to have lawful authority for these actions (Viva Network 2000:14).

Certainly this next attempt to rid the streets of children is not officially endorsed by any government. Larry Sharp in the forward to *Street Children*, describes the chilling world scene regarding community children: there are close to 100 million children living on the streets. Sharp goes on to say, "Documented evidence shows that merchants, hired mercenaries and even police . . . are methodically attacking, torturing and even killing children they find on the streets" (Sharp 1997:2). Children have been killed in a number of countries by off-duty police officers and other vigilante groups. The Associated Press released documents stating the killing of several "street kids" in Rio de Janeiro (July 24, 1993). Seven children ages eight to twelve were murdered by a group of men composed of some police officers. This incident, of police killing children, is certainly not the first nor is it the last time this has been documented. The Associated Press ran a news release that stated, "A 1992 Brazilian congressional investigation found that more than 4,600 street children had been killed in the previous three years" (July 24, 1993). From my personal journal entry on November 2, 1995, I describe the following account of injustice:

> Sunday's paper told us about a street kid that had been killed and we were told that the morgue called the church as well about [Carlos] being killed. After more articles on Monday and a few phone calls we found out that it was true. [Carlos] had been hit in the head with a bat or pipe and killed. The funeral was Monday night . . . it was horrible. It was terrible to see him in the casket

and it didn't even look like him at all. I now grieve for [Carlos], I don't know if he is with the Savior. The best thing is if he is with Christ, he is in JOY and PEACE.

This injustice has occurred in many parts of the world, including Mozambique, where children have reported being beaten and kicked by police as they sleep (Vincent 1995:4).

Satan is at work, seeking to infiltrate political structures and work through them to destroy the lives of community children. Just as the enemy can get strongholds in the lives of individuals, it seems that he can gain strongholds in the structures as well. When children are killed by off-duty police officers (whose duty is to protect), we see that Satan has perverted the very nature of such groups with evil intent.

SOCIAL STRUCTURES

Social structures (i.e. religious institutions, governmental systems, public services, etc.), which God has meant for good, can in fact be influenced by demons.[13] Scripture tells us: *"For it was the Father's good pleasure for all the fullness to dwell in Him, and through Him to reconcile all things to Himself, having made peace through the blood of His cross; through Him, I say, whether things on earth or things in heaven"* (NASB Colossians 1:19-20).

13- Peter Wagner says "social structures are not, in themselves, demonic, but they can be and often are demonized by some extremely pernicious and dominating demonic personalities, which I call territorial spirits" (1992:96).

Yes, God desires to restore all things unto Himself, including worldly structures. Walter Wink refers to these systems that control and destroy as the "Domination System."[14] Ephesians 6:12 is the base text for the concept of *"powers"* in the New Testament. Scripture clearly teaches that our struggle is not against people in government or other public services, but rather against the demonic forces and the unjust system itself that continues to create injustices, including those that affect community children.

The systems that God has given us for organization and for maintaining some justice in our world have at some point seemingly been corrupted. In light of the topic at hand, I have no doubt that the contribution of demonic activity and sin are at work seeking to set up oppressive structures that create huge problems for community children and other poor families who live under the service of this world.

Community children are powerless and have been used by public entities as well as individuals with ties to political and other institutional systems. One example of this can be seen during election year. In most countries where there are community children present, politicians will not hesitate to gain a vote by referring to their efforts to help children that are at risk and on the street. I recently witnessed a scene where a child, sleeping on the street, was approached by a politician and given special treatment, with the media in tow. Where are the politicians when it really comes to providing a solution to help these children over the long run? Many of them are certainly not

---

14- In his book, Engaging the Powers, Wink refers to Ephesians 6:12 in describing the "powers" as part of the very domination system itself (1992:42).

to be found among the children that take up the street corners. As has been noted, these social systems can be demonic, with evil beings empowering the injustice, but most can certainly be human powered as well.

The main concept of demonic and evil structures in Scripture can be found in the word *cosmos* (world). Ronald Sider provides the following insight:

> In Greek thought, the word cosmos referred to the structures of civilized life, especially the patterns of the Greek city-state that were viewed as essentially good. But the biblical writers knew that sin had invaded and distorted the structures and values of society (1997:117).

Sin has certainly distorted the goodness of these systems. Scripture tells us:

> *Do not love the world or things in the world. The Love of the Father is not in those who love the world; for all that is in the world — the desires of the flesh, the desires of the eyes, the pride of riches — -comes not from the Father but from the world. And the world and its desires are passing away, but those who do the will of God live forever (1 John 2:15-17 NRSV).*

As believers, we are exhorted not to live according to the desires of this world. Why? Because the desires of this world are full of sin and are corrupted based on what we are told here in 1 John.

When was the last time you heard this teaching in church? These are important issues that we as street educators must begin to consider. Teaching on structural injustice and sin is perhaps the great omission of the church today (Sider 1997:110).

Clearly there is a spiritual battle taking place for the social structures in any given society. Satan is most definitely behind some political, religious and economic structures seeking to take control of them to use for his own purposes. Christians must take a stand and be involved in using the structures for God's kingdom and no longer allowing demonic forces to rule. How we as Christians actually go about this, is the topic I would now like to discuss.

RESPONDING TO STRONGHOLDS

Jeff Anderson, in his manual on reaching community children says, "Let's unite our forces throughout [the world] and launch a massive offensive attack against the strongholds of Satan" (1995:8.1). I couldn't agree more, but how are we to do this? I believe that there are many ways that we can confront both personal and systemic strongholds, but two primary ones will be looked at here. The two primary responses within the context of working with community children are *intercesory prayer* and *changing perceptions*.

INTERCESSORY PRAYER

God is calling His Community to intercede for destitute children in both prayer and changing societies' attitudes towards such children. To intercede means to pray on one's behalf and to stand in the gap for the person we are praying for. The Church is called to intercede for neglected children all over the world. We must respond in prayer for the some 100 million children on the street worldwide.

As believers we must be the ones who seek God for the restitution that is due these children. Many organizations have seen a very low percentage of children actually leave the street. I believe one reason for this is that there has not been an essential breakthrough in the lives of the children. Satan has been allowed to take strongholds in the lives of the children and perhaps even the geographical areas where they live and sleep. What would happen if, instead of meeting to discuss problems we encounter, we prayed for the problems and issues and asked God to intervene? What would happen if we took an hour to pray before going out to contact the children on the street?

We must pray and ask for God to intervene on the structural injustices occurring in our world today. If we aspire to have an effect upon the "social order"- and I certainly do - then we ought to turn to God in prayer, asking that He act and bring healing to the structures and to the lives of the children.

This type of prayer includes going to God and asking Him to attack and destroy the strongholds that have been allowed to develop. This prayer is claiming the victory that Christ has won on Calvary.

As Christian workers we will receive our strength through prayer and praise. The war is real and as kingdom servants we need to recognize that it is Satan that is holding these children in captivity. The responsibility to free them has been given to the Church. The street is often personified as if it had the power to hold these children, but as Christians we recognize there is another source.

In making contact with the youth on the street, we have found it helpful first to follow a child for a few minutes and pray for him or her. After we spend some time praying we will make contact with him or her. As an organization we also have a policy that states those who go to the street to contact the children should do so with at least one other individual. This automatically provides a prayer partner who prays as the other makes the contact and does most of the talking. Prayer cannot be overemphasized!

PRAYER WALKS

Prayer walks consist of walking through the areas with a group and seeking God and asking Him to redeem and restore the social structures and systems for His purposes. God delights in redeeming His creation (Colossians 1:19-20). Is there something inherently evil about the political process in any given country? No! It is certainly possible that Satan has twisted the *"powers"* to serve his own desires, but God, in partnership with His Church, desires to change and redeem that which rightly belongs to Him.

CHANGING PERCEPTIONS

Recently I ran into Eduardo and Jesús. As I walked by where they were seated, I didn't even notice them due to the crowds that were already taking over the street. From somewhere behind me I heard, "Gregorio." When I turned around I saw them, sitting in front of a bakery. Eduardo was covered with scars from head to toe while Jesús had been spared from such markings. Jesús was always known as the "beggar" for he would often beg for the others due to his young and innocent appearance. We talked for a few minutes about Johnny, a boy who died a day prior to this meeting after having fallen from a tall wall while high on crack cocaine. We talked about the importance of life and the need to come into contact with our Creator and Savior. I then offered to buy them breakfast, which they did not hesitate to accept. As we turned and walked into the bakery to make our purchase, the man behind the counter refused us. The man said "no food for those two." Why this man was so angry with the two I have no idea, but not wanting to cause a commotion I walked away, wanting to try my luck next door. The next place sold me the food without a hassle. After the boys left, I returned to the prior place where we were rejected, to look into the situation a little. I was confronted by several men who told me "what those guys need is not food but rather poison." I couldn't believe what I had just heard. As I left the bakery the words kept echoing in my head.... "Poison," why would anyone deserve this kind of response, I wondered. The hatred those people had towards the young men was frightening.

Another important aspect of our ministry to the community child is the task of changing perceptions or attitudes. Unfortunately, many people in different societies have been corrupted into thinking that all community children are bad. This is simply not true! Many people have come to look at children living on the street as disposable, as trash. As Christians we have the responsibility to change that way of thinking. Community children have become scapegoats in many societies. They are considered the essence of the problem that many cities are having with theft and assaults. Is this really true? I think not. The rationalization that these children are the reason that there is theft on our cities' streets is ridiculous! If we must find a scapegoat let's look to the social structure that has allowed them (or even encouraged them) to take to the street.

One way to change attitudes is to involve people in society in the community child project. What would happen if we included several police officers, some store merchants, neighbors, etc., in painting the drop-in-center along with the children themselves? Certainly they would learn that these children are not trash and are very capable of loving and laughing just like they do. Another way of encouraging this "attitude adjustment" is by inviting community leaders and others to an open house of the drop-in-center or project. Getting people in touch with the children themselves is one positive way to change attitudes. Participative involvement will move mountains if we allow space for it.

THE WAR IS REAL

Sadly, it is clear that Satan is devouring many young people today. The strategies that the adversary has used include such things as abuse, poverty, drug addiction and police brutality. The enemy is at work, seeking to destroy the lives of young people. There is a war being waged. Although Christ won the victory at Calvary when He died for our sins, Satan continues to be a menace, seeking to destroy as many children as he can. While we must be careful to acknowledge the pain that individual children sustain as a result of this "war," we must also take courage and place our trust in Christ for the victory.

7

CHILDREN'S RIGHTS AND ADVOCACY

Walking to the office each morning is an experience in itself. Our office is located in downtown Caracas, on the famous boulevard called *Sabana Grande*. Anyone familiar with *Sabana Grande* will tell you before you visit, "be careful and keep your hands on your wallet or purse." Just a few years ago, *Sabana Grande* was mainly a shopping area for the working class person. Today, *Sabana Grande* is filled with *"buhoneros,"* (street venders) and the homeless. On most weekdays the boulevard is filled with venders selling anything from incense to blue jeans. Most of these venders arrive each morning and slowly take over the boulevard with their stands and products. It can prove to be difficult walking from one end of the strip to the other due to the amount of venders and pedestrians. Amongst the people are the *"malandros"* and *"huelepegas,"* the street thieves and street kids (glue sniffers).

On one occasion, the street outreach team went looking for some boys on the *Sabana Grande* boulevard we had promised to take to a park for the day. We told them to meet us on a particular corner and to wait for us. Upon arrival I can remember watching in shock as three police officers beat up two of the boys by repeatedly kicking them. They kicked them for nothing more than just loitering on a street corner. When a colleague tried to intervene the police threatened my friend and took his identification papers. Soon enough a number of us had arrived on the scene and the police left the area.

What can we do to confront this type of abuse I wondered? As Christians, we believe that all people are created in the image of God and have individual rights. What kind of response can we have towards those who actually carry out these acts of abuse and killings? As Christians we await the kingdom of God and the justice of God, but can we not do something now on earth to respond to such acts of injustice? I believe we can!

I have chosen to write about the rights of children in this section for two reasons. 1) There is a misconception that human rights is only a political discussion not meant for Christians and 2) I believe that human rights can be used in a proper manner and can benefit Christian ministry. So I really want to persuade those that feel that human rights are useless. Many feel that a belief in human dignity is the Christian's version of "human rights," and thus we have no need for a human-driven rights-based program. I hope to show why the concept behind child rights is important and how we as Christian workers in the field of child-care ministries can use this important tool.

In working with these children, we must first recognize that they are children and as such, have certain rights. These rights are recognized by both inter-governmental and non-governmental organizations such as the United Nations, World Vision and the Viva Network (see the United Nations Convention on the Rights of Children and The Oxford Statement on Children at Risk), but God in the Bible highlights these rights as well. Certainly what Jesus states, *"I have come that they may have life, and have it to the full,"* (note NASV translation, *"abundant life"*)[15] is a powerful expression of God's concern for all of humankind, including the homeless child. The child on the street has the right to an abundant life through Christ. This *"abundant life"* certainly includes meeting the basic necessities of human life, including family, food, housing and love.

HUMAN RIGHTS

What exactly are human rights? On December 10, 1948, the General Assembly of the United Nations accepted and adopted the Universal Declaration of Human Rights in response to the atrocities that were witnessed during the Second World War. What followed was monumental, because up to that point there had been no international law protecting the rights and freedoms of all humankind. Once the declaration was accepted, the main assembly of the United Nations called upon each member state to disseminate the information throughout their particular

15- John 10:10.

country via schools and other educational institutions. The declaration set forth basic rights and freedoms for all women, men and children.

Included in these basic rights are political and civil rights, as well as the right to have "freedom from slavery, from torture, from arbitrary arrest and from interference with family; the right to recognition before the law; the right to a fair trial; the right to marry and have a family; and the right to freedom of thought and peaceful assembly" (UNICEF Internet source: A Background Note on Human Rights in General).

Out of the Universal Declaration of Human Rights came other declarations, such as: The Convention on the Rights of the Child; The International Covenant on Civil and Political Rights; The Convention against Torture and other Forms of Cruel, Inhuman or Degrading Treatment; as well as regional conventions such as the American Convention on Human Rights and the African Charter on Human and People's Rights.

THE CONVENTION ON THE RIGHTS OF THE CHILD (CRC)

The Convention on the Rights of the Child was written over a period of ten years, with the help and insight of various experts from different ethnic and religious backgrounds. Once the convention was accepted and adopted by the General Assembly (with representatives from every country of the world) it was then approved as international law. The CRC was adopted on November 20, 1989 and it was fully ratified in 1990 with 122 countries in agreement. As has been widely publicized, only the United States (due to the belief that current U.S. law was sufficient) and Somalia (due to political conflict and lack of government) refused to ratify the document. The convention focuses on four main areas, which are: 1) survival rights, 2) development rights, 3) protection rights and 4) participation rights (Grant 1992:2). Upon signing the CRC, the individual country agrees, generally speaking, with the spirit of the CRC and agrees to move towards ratification. Ratification takes place as each country agrees to apply international law to national policy and accept in full, the responsibility of implementing the CRC in its particular country. It also must be accepted by the country's parliament, congress, king or ruling authority in order to be ratified into law.

The CRC and other international human rights laws have been set up to protect the rights of children and adults from states. That is: "Both states and individuals are subjects of international human rights laws. Only states (or non-state entities that have the powers of states) can violate a person's human rights, but it is also up to the state to protect these rights" (Byrne 1998:4). The state is to protect the rights of each individual and in no way violate those same rights. But what happens when a representative of that very "protective agency" violates its responsibility? They must address the violation with local courts and authorities first. If this is not possible, then the international rights law provides the resources to do so via international mechanisms (Byrne 1998:4).

Let's take a look at what the CRC actually says. While it is not possible to go article by article through the contents of the CRC, I will outline a couple pertinent statements that can be useful to Christians reaching community children and others at risk. I encourage you to read through your own copy of the CRC.

ARTICLE 3

1. In all actions concerning children, whether under-taken by public or private social welfare institutions, courts of law, administrative authorities or legislative bodies, the best interests of the child shall be a primary consideration.

The priority of the child is in focus here. What will our ministries look like if we keep the child's best interest in mind? To heed priority to the child keeps us on the same road with Jesus. We have seen Jesus' response to children and have been encouraged to follow that road, but now the UN has also seen the need to think positively and pro-actively in our response to children. What would our world look like if the countries of our world took this one article seriously? To implement this law and to hold people accountable who do not keep the interests of children in mind is perhaps the most difficult part. To hold accountable police who do not follow this international law is a great need. To hold accountable government run homes where children simply become numbers and are neglected is of utmost importance.

ARTICLE 6

1. States Parties recognize that every child has the inherent right to life.
2. States Parties shall ensure to the maximum extent possible the survival and development of the child.

Inherent right to life is very important to us as Christians. Children living in the street have a right to develop and live long lives. Children living far below the poverty line have a right to survival and development. Once again we see children receiving the priority they deserve as children of God, with inherent rights to life. Implementation and accountability for those who violate this article must become a priority for us in the Christian church.

These two articles alone certainly are not convincing that the Church should blindly adopt the CRC as truth, but my hope is that we will at least consider the possibility that we can now look into this important international document and find a tool that will help us in our God given obligation to care for community children and other children at risk.

THE OXFORD STATEMENT: A CHRISTIAN RESPONSE

The Oxford Statement is the product of a consultation that took place in January of 1997 with 58 representatives from 38 organizations in Africa, Asia, Europe, and North and

Latin America. The consultation took place in Oxford, England, and was sponsored by the Viva Network and the Oxford Centre for World Missions.

This declaration is a good example of how the Community can and should declare that children have rights and deserve protection. While the Oxford Statement rightfully upholds the cause of children at risk, it is not intended to be a legal document, as is the CRC, but rather a Christian response and declaration that God loves and desires to protect children at risk. Just as there are children's rights that are recognized by such organizations as the United Nations, the Oxford Statement declares that children at risk deserve our attention and advocacy but from a Christian world view. The purpose is given to the declaration when it states, "It is for the neglected and exploited children of our generation that our hearts cry out. We can no longer stand by and watch them suffer and die in their millions while their enemies are left free to stalk them on every side" (chapter 1.0). Just as we sought several examples in how to go about using the CRC in our ministries, so too we must consider how we can use the Oxford Statement.

My personal thoughts are that this document can best be used in declaring to the world the Church's response in the midst of the crisis. For too long the Christian Church has been silent; for too long we have not spoken up for children at risk. This Christian declaration can be used to show the world that we are deeply concerned about these children. We can also use the statement to promote child advocacy in our churches and in our educational institutions.

Take, for example, a statement found in section 2.3,

which says, "The largest cause of death amongst children is malnutrition. Tens of thousands die every day as a result of curable diseases caused by simple nutritional deficiencies." A simple declaration about malnutrition can awaken the Church to get involved with this issue. The declaration also recognizes such truths as "government complicity and corruption." In section 2.9, the Statement declares, "The promotion of the welfare of every citizen is a responsibility of government." The statement goes on to say, "Corruption in governments has also led to child trafficking, sexual exploitation of children and child labor." The truth needs to be heard no matter whose feet we step on. How are we doing as a Church in dealing with government corruption? Is it our place to deal with this? It is if it affects the well being of people. The light exposes the darkness and we certainly are the light.

The Oxford Statement also focuses in on some theological foundations for working with children at risk. Take for example section 3.1. This section is called, "The Biblical Significance of the Child." God's Word is absolute and there can be no dispute that He gives priority to the at-risk child. To defend the homeless and abused child is to stand with God in defending His people. This declaration needs to be made to the Church and society.

Another declaration that is made by the statement refers to the necessity of the family. Section 3.2 says, "We affirm that God's basic societal unit is the family (Gen 2:24; 5:21-6:4) which God has ordained as based upon a man and a woman living in faithfulness to one another and the offspring with which He blesses that union (Psalm 127:3-5)." This is something that the Church must focus on. The family unit plays an important role in preventing children from becoming at risk. We do way too little in working with families at risk. As the statement in section 3.2 says, "family disintegration and dysfunction invariably results in children at risk." To prevent children from becoming at risk, we must focus on the family and train the family in such a way as to equip it to run as God has intended.

The statement includes what churches and Christian organizations are currently doing and recommendations for the future. I have chosen to include recommendations for the future in full, due to the fact that this message needs to get out! Churches throughout the world have a window of opportunity and we must respond to this prophetic word that has been urged upon us by this group of men and women.

ALL CHURCHES have a responsibility to search for and implement tangible structures by which they can effectively minister to children at risk both locally and globally. We recommend that they:

- make themselves aware of the crisis;
- make themselves aware of what other people and ministries are currently doing;
- set aside both financial and people resources, in order to link with and participate in specific ministry programs;
- regularly pray within the congregational worship service for children at risk;
- ensure that children at risk and their families are welcomed into and welcome in the church community;
- encourage children to participate in worship and ministry;
- provide a sense of significance, emotional acceptance and support for care givers.

ALL GRASS-ROOTS MINISTRIES (whether run by local churches or particular organizations) should seek to reinforce forms of interconnectedness in their common endeavors to minister effectively to children in their community. We recommend that local, regional and international networks be encouraged by the development of facilitators and networkers in a servant hearted capacity. These various networks could serve the body of Christ by identifying those who are involved in doing creative ministries, though often isolated and unknown, so that these smaller groups have access to shared information, resources and encouragement. Mutual support and mutually shared resources should be encouraged at all levels.

ALL CHRISTIAN AGENCIES supporting work with children at risk should be committed to improving the quality of existing efforts through the sharing of ideas, information and resources, as well as through training and the development of meaningful structures of accountability.

THE CHRISTIAN COMMUNITY must raise a voice for and along with children to call to account those in positions of economic and government power who make and implement laws and policies that abuse, ignore, or take advantage of children at risk. This will involve increased participation in forums recommending and implementing social policy toward children at risk.

HUMAN RIGHTS: THE CHRISTIAN DEBATE

William Carey, "the father of modern missions," is well

known for his opposition of widow burning in India during his stay as a missionary there. Carey, who was born in a poor family in 1761, went to India as a missionary to bring people to Christ. Carey, among other pursuits, defended the rights of countless women who were doomed to burn along with their fallen husbands.

Gary Haugen (1999), in his book, *Good News about Injustice* lists numerous stories of Christians standing up against human rights abuses throughout history. One story that captured my attention was the work of Jessie Daniel Ames, a white woman who stood up against lynching of African-Americans in the United States. We're told that in just four years, "from 1918 to 1921, twenty-eight African-Americans were burned at the stake by mob action. As late as the 1940s lynching was still a common method of social control and intimidation in the southern states" (1999:57).

In 1930, before the Universal Declaration of Human Rights was even written, Ames and a group of eleven other concerned women created the Association of Southern Women for the Prevention of Lynching (ASWPL). These women were Christians and took their cause back to their churches. By the early 1940s, over one hundred women's associations representing close to 4 million women supported the work of the ASWPL. These women were key to preventing the lynching of numerous African-Americans during their time (1999:57-59).

Christians have been involved with upholding human rights for centuries, even before the concept was put into writing by the United Nations.

Christians have been upholding these human rights because of the fundamental belief that all humans have been created in the image of God (Gen. 1:26-30). Some argue that our motivation for doing so is based on the uniqueness and dignity of humans. This is true! It is because of our Creator and our uniqueness as humans that all people deserve to be treated with respect and justice. Charles R. Taber in his article, "In the Image of God: the Gospel and Human Rights," argues that human rights, as they stand today, are a western-influenced grouping of specific items that have lost their roots from Scripture (2002:100-101). It is certainly true that our motive for doing good works and upholding that which is right must be based in Scripture. It is correct that the modern concept of human rights is imperfect and can in fact be proven to work against itself at times, but it must also not be forgotten that Christian child-care workers can use this imperfect tool to make an impact on our world today. Use of the CRC, and the resulting national law may in fact be the only wording that will be taken seriously in a court of law. If we are to gain respect as a legitimate caretaker of community children, we must be respectful of law and the CRC in our respective countries. In some cases, not to be respectful will amount to illegal action on the part of caring and sincere Christians.

Paul Stephenson in the book *Celebrating Children* covers thoroughly the debate between the Christian worldview and human rights. Stephenson argues that human rights help us to maintain religious freedom and values. He believes, that for people of faith, human rights are the result of our relationships with one another and with God (Miles and Wright 2003:60). Our motivation for upholding children's rights should be based upon God's concern for children that are at risk in our world today. Scripture is clear.

Children should be cared for as unique and created in the image of God, with dignity and individual rights. When a state or authority violates these rights, it should be held accountable because of the infraction. The Community needs to uphold rights no matter what the cost.

THE CHURCH AND HER CHILDREN

We can use child right laws to further the kingdom of God on earth. One tool that can be used to extend God's reign is the principle that humans have basic inherent rights and that children, those most vulnerable in our society, should be protected. Specifically, the Community is called to be God's "hands and feet" in extending the kingdom of God to children through advocacy and outreach.

ADVOCACY

I recently met up with one of the older boys we work with. It had been quite a while since I had seen Eduardo. He had turned 18, which meant he was no longer a minor and could be incarcerated as an adult if caught stealing. We discussed this for a while, for he very well knew the consequences of what the "*cárcel*" means here. Jail is certainly no free ticket in Venezuela. As we discussed his future and what his plans were, we decided to get a cola at a local cafe. The owner was not happy to see us. It took some time to convince this man that our intent was only to drink a cola and talk.

I am always amazed at the lack of respect others have for youth that are on the street, both in their words and actions. To say that children and youth on the street are frowned upon is an understatement.

God defends and calls upon us to stand up for these children (and young people) that are in crisis. If the Christian Church does not stand up and defend homeless youth, then who will stand for them? Generally speaking, some societies have been indifferent to community children. This attitude must not be allowed in the Community. Advocacy is an important means to provide protection for the homeless child.

ADVOCACY: WHAT DOES IT INVOLVE?

- Advocacy is an integral component of development work
- Advocacy is not necessarily confrontational
- Advocacy needs to deal with root causes
- Advocacy is usually involved with ensuring justice in policies and practice
- Advocacy is strengthened by accurate information and experience (Atkins & Gordon 1999:3).

In Proverbs 31:8-9 believers are commanded to, "*Speak up for those who cannot speak for themselves, for the rights of all who are destitute. Speak up and judge fairly; defend the rights of the poor and needy.*" Children on the street are poor and needy, thus the Church is to stand up for them, whether it be in court or on the street before police and vigilante groups. These children are certainly among those that cannot "*speak for themselves.*" An advocate is simply someone who intercedes, protects and cares for others in their time of need. Kilbourn suggests the following ideas for practical advocacy:

- Raising public awareness through such means as posters, educative methods, rallies, peaceful demonstrations, mobile theater groups (including children's theater groups), marches;
- Initiating boycotts (such as against those supplying glue to children or shopkeepers who mistreat children);
- Provoking debate and discussion through media (newspapers, newsletters and other print media, radio, television, videos) about children's problems and issues;
- Seeking reforms through political lobbying and letter writing campaigns (1997:225).

Some other ideas include:

- Training of public and private organizations working with community children (detention centers, police forces, etc.);
- Training the children themselves in their rights and the laws of the land;
- Establishing a legal defense for community children;
- Encouraging local churches to get behind these children and to take a stand for them.

Just as we are to intercede for these children before God, so we ought to intercede and defend them in the name of Jesus before the social systems that keep them in bondage.

OUTREACH

By outreach I mean, going to children on the street, in prisons, in their homes and inviting them into the community and family of God. The kingdom of God is invitational, not coercive. A powerful call for outreach is revealed to us in Scripture. In Matthew 25, Jesus tells us that when we minister to people, or in our case, community children, we are in fact ministering to Christ Himself. Once again, thinking through the human rights' model, especially article 6:2 of the CRC, we must ask ourselves, would we place Christ into an enclosed, high walled, barbed-wire detention center, with little access to education, in order to help him develop? No! Is the lack of funding any excuse for not allowing a child to develop appropriately? Of course it is not!

> *Then the King will say to those on his right, 'Come, you who are blessed by my father; take your inheritance, the kingdom prepared for you since the creation of the world. For I was hungry and you gave me something to eat, I was thirsty and you gave me something to drink, I was a stranger and you invited me in, I needed clothes and you clothed me, I was sick and you looked after me, I was in prison and you came to visit me.' Then the righteous will answer him, 'Lord, when did we see you hungry and feed you, or thirsty and give you something to drink? When did we see you a stranger and invite you in, or needing clothes and clothe you? When did we see you sick or in prison and go to visit you?' The King will reply, 'I tell you the truth, whatever you did for one of the least of these brothers of mine, you did for me' (Matthew 25:34-40).*

Kingdom citizens see community children and young people in the personhood of Christ. It is in these verses that we see a clear and descriptive picture of the coming King and His judgment. The homeless child is a figure of Christ Himself and outreach must consist of meeting the physical needs of these children.

God, in using His instrument, the Church, brings hope to the afflicted child. What a privilege it is to be used of God to bring life and joy to that which was dead and hopeless. In light of Matthew 25, it is quite apparent that Believers should be sharing their resources with those who are in need.

Outreach will look different depending upon the context and child. Some programs of outreach involve counseling, education, housing, praying, etc. Outreach, whether in the form of exchanging clean clothes for dirty ones, feeding children who need nutritious meals or building a home for community children is crucial if we are to extend the kingdom *"here on earth as it is in heaven."*

If we are to be influential in our defense of children and really see this population all over the world set free, the Community must be involved in reaching them through advocacy and outreach. The Church is God's instrument for extending His kingdom and as such, we have the responsibility to reach out in the love of Jesus Christ.

If it takes applying the CRC and holding public officials accountable, then that is what we must do. If it takes making our churches and fellow brethren aware of the need to work with children at risk by using the Oxford Statement, then I say, we must do it. The Lord has provided tools for us to protect and defend the rights of children. Now it is our decision to use what He has given us.

For too long the evangelical Church has missed a great opportunity in using human rights to promote child protection. We must not fail in our pursuit of justice for those without a voice in our world, but rather heed the call that has been sent forth to us. As the Community of

God, we have been given certain tools to alleviate suffering in this world. The concept behind human rights is that it is simply a tool that has been systematized to help us defend people in need, especially through legal means (World Vision 2002:17). These tools are available today for our use. May we not be neglectful in using them.

8

A MOVEMENT OF GOD

God is moving powerfully, using His Church like never before in reaching out to all children at risk. He is certainly calling His Church to respond to the needs of the *"least of these."* In the midst of so many appalling circumstances on the street, God is at work in His kingdom and He is using His People to extend it forcefully.

HISTORICAL STREAMS OF GOD AT WORK

Many Christians have been reaching out to abandoned children for centuries. A child living on the street is nothing new. Andy Butcher notes street living children have been documented as far back as ancient times (Kilbourn 1996: 23). Many single women missionaries were known for taking in children that were wandering the streets. Ruth Tucker says, "Not infrequently the missionaries who took these children in were single women who had repressed their motherly instincts and were subconscious-ly eager to substitute unwanted children for the children of their own they were denied" (Tucker 1988:129). Throughout Christian history we see people like Emma Whittmore and Amy Carmichael ministering in the name of Jesus. Certainly there were many others who minis-tered (i.e. George Müeller and Lillian Trasher), yet these women are two primary examples of Christians minister-ing to needy children.

Amy Carmichael is known for her many years of work with children in India. Much of her work focused on rescuing girls from temple prostitution. Sherwood Eddy in describing her outreach, wrote:

> The number of children about to be dedicated [to Hindu gods] who were rescued by miss Carmichael now runs into several thousands . . . There are now, in 1945, over eight hundred children in her three homes. Each institution is at once a Christian home, a school, and a center for character building (Tucker 1988:135).

Carmichael's work became known as the Dohnavur fellowship. Two decades after her work began, thirty care centers were set up to take in children. Like work today with community children, the work she accomplished was not done without obstacles. Many Hindus were against her work in rescuing the very children they had placed in the temples, while other missionaries felt that she was presenting a deterrent to true evangelism by involving herself in such work. Despite the obstacles, the ministry in which she was involved received internation-al attention and praise (Tucker 1988:136).

Another good example of God moving His Church to

work among unwanted children is seen in the work of Emma Whittmore. Whittmore founded the Door of Hope mission to street girls. Her first home was established in 1890 in New York City but by the time of her death in 1931 she had nearly one hundred homes in cities around the world. Many of the girls with whom Whittmore worked, later went on to become missionaries themselves, reaching people in the New York city slums (Tucker 1988:79).

A NEW SENSE OF URGENCY

While Christians have understood God's heart for children for quite some time, it was not until recently, that large numbers of people have come together to discuss strategies for reaching these children. There is a new sense of urgency to help children in crises. Groups such as the Lausanne Committee for evangelization and the AD2000 and Beyond Movement have pulled large numbers of people together to address evangelistic challenges, yet few, until recently, have done so with just children at risk or community children in mind.

In 1995 I had the privilege of attending one of the first conferences organized by the Viva Network. The conference was held in San José, Costa Rica with 38 people representing 23 organizations from 10 different nations. The goal of the conference was to encourage Christian workers to evangelize children at risk by working together. As a result of the conference, national networks of people working with children at risk began to form. The Viva Network currently has 66 network initiatives in 43 countries, linking together 16,000 workers that are reaching

160,000 children. The Viva Network is pulling together people and organizations from around the world and encouraging them to network in working with children at risk. Praise God for this!

God has prompted certain individuals to write books and articles concerning children and the need to minister to them. Phyllis Kilbourn has edited a number of books dealing with community children and other children at risk.[16] Other, non-Christian authors and researchers have begun to write about the plight of homeless children. Their books and articles have been useful to Christians in coming to a better understanding on reaching out to such children.[17]

There are numerous examples throughout the world where Christian churches and organizations are ministering powerfully and with much success. God is pulling Believers together to discuss and consult about reaching community children for Christ.

THE TRANSFORMATION WITHIN

While there are many examples of God transforming children who lived on the street into servants of the King, the following are just some samples of fruit. I believe that God wants to raise up an army of former street living children to minister in boldness and power to the future generations of community youth. Not only are these young peo-

---

16- See bibliography.
17- Despite the fact that they are "non-Christian," they have much to say in regards to treatment and intervention.

ple able to identify with community children, but they are an example of the power of God. One of the goals in our ministry is to involve those kids who graduate from the program into the lives of the children who are just starting the program. There is a tremendous need for godly men and women who have experienced life on the street to disciple and mentor younger children.

DOUGLAS

One of the first boys I met back in 1995 on the street was a thirteen-year-old named Douglas. Since 1995 Douglas has gone through some severe trials in his life. In his younger years, pre-street life, Douglas lived with his mom and stepfather. They lived in a very poor neighborhood on the outskirts of Caracas. Douglas was sent to the streets of this mega-city to beg. If he returned with enough money, he would be patted on the head and be told "good boy," but if he returned with less than the desired amount, he would be hit and cursed at.

Douglas made a decision one day to stay on the streets for good, to leave behind his life of abuse and to seek out an existence for himself on the mean streets of Caracas. Douglas spent most of his time high on drugs and stealing food and other things he wanted. On occasion, when he and his friends were really desperate for food, they would throw dead mice onto tables seated outside so that dinner goers would abandon their meals quickly, only to give the kids time to grab the food and run. One day, while making contact with the boys on the boulevard a colleague and I ran into him. Douglas immediately showed us some sores he had on his stomach, which later turned out to be scabies. After taking him to see a Doctor, Douglas was desperate to leave the street, so we invited him to the Lighthouse Ranch. Over time Douglas healed physically, but the years of abuse and street life made it hard for him to heal emotionally. The street still called out to him. One evening while cleaning one of the boy's rooms, I noticed a knife under Douglas' mattress. Douglas became so accustomed to having to protect himself; he still felt the need to have a weapon.

While living at the Lighthouse Ranch, Douglas began to show an interest in God and committed his life to Him. He grew in his relationship with the Lord, yet still struggled with obeying the house rules and structure. While he was living with us, we heard the sad news of one boy's death on the street. Many of us from the ministry made our way over to the funeral home where the boy was being mourned. The group of boys with whom Douglas had spent most of his time on the street also came to the funeral. Douglas powerfully proclaimed the Gospel to the boys that night. He shared about what God had done for him and how much the Lord loves each one of them.

As the months went by, Douglas grew in his relationship with the Lord, but always struggled with accepting the love that he was being shown by his house parents and the other staff members. After living at the Lighthouse Ranch for approximately six months he left to return to the street. During that year Douglas was in and out of government institutions and group homes where abuse and mistreatment were not uncommon.

A year after he had left, Douglas came back to us and was received at the Ranch with open arms. Douglas started where he had left off. He began to grow in his relationship with the Lord once again, memorizing Scripture and sharing new passages he had found with anyone who would listen. Douglas was sent off to learn a trade in animal husbandry and agriculture. He returned to the Ranch with his newfound skills and began to implement a chicken hatchery to help feed the boys living there. After several months, Douglas decided he would return home, the very home he left many years before. Like many feared, Douglas wandered back to his old stomping grounds and old friends. While spending some time with some of his old buddies on the street, a group of them were arrested for robbery. Douglas and some of his other friends were sent to prison because of their age. He was eighteen now and there was no way out like in his earlier days of being in youth detention centers. What he experienced in jail, those of us on the outside can only imagine. Douglas has described it as hell. While in jail he recommitted his life to Christ and moved into the Christian section where he was baptized and once again, memorized and studied Scripture. After serving two years, a judge was contacted regarding his case and he was eventually released into our care, under special regulations.

Douglas has been at the Ranch, serving children and youth for over three years since he was released. He is now on staff with *Niños de la Luz*, married and has two beautiful boys. Douglas and his bride, Ismerling, are now committed believers seeking to restore other children who come from at-risk situations. Douglas would be the first to say that his journey is not over, but all of us around him, testifying to what the Lord is doing in his life *would* be the first to say that God is at work, using him in powerful ways. Recently, Douglas shared his testimony to a predominately non-Christian audience at a benefit dinner. He shared about his faith in Christ and his desire to serve his Lord. Many of the 350 people in attendance were moved to tears by his wonderful story and responded with a standing ovation as Douglas went back to his seat.

The Father of the fatherless is at work, raising up many young people throughout the world that come out of difficult backgrounds. I believe that He takes great pleasure in displaying His children to the world. Similar to how He is using Douglas to make an impact in Caracas, Venezuela, the Lord is moving in sometimes surprising ways, yet always triumphant ways.

MARLON

Another example of God at work on the street in the lives of community children and youth is a young man named Marlon. Marlon was involved in a street gang in Manila, Philippines. He was also involved in prostitution, which helped him to buy food and drugs. Marlon went in and out of rehabilitation centers for a number of years. At age twelve he was caught in committing armed robbery and was placed under arrest. When he and the other boys tried to resist, two of his friends were killed by the police. The police turned on him, beat him with a revolver and then handcuffed him to a Jeepney (a large Jeep used for transportation). While the police were distracted Marlon escaped, saving his life (Monsma 1993:1-2).

Monsma says, "Today Marlon is still running . . . but a very different race! ' . . . run in such a way that you may win' (1 Cor. 9:24). With a life transformed by God's love, Marlon is running the race of life for Jesus Christ" (1993:2). After many years on the street, Marlon is now ministering and directing a kid's club in one area of Manila (Monsma 1993:1-2).

FROM "STREET CHILD" TO MISSIONARY

For several years now, *Niños de la Luz* team members have periodically been going on short-term mission trips to the Amazon region of Venezuela, accompanied by ex-street dwelling children, ministering together and fulfilling the great commission (Matthew 28:19-20) and the great commandment (Matthew 22:37-40). Where this will take us, no one knows, but we are certain that God is using these teenagers to extend His kingdom. The following account details one of those trips among the Piaröa indigenous community.

After a 13 hour bus ride we arrived into the town of Puerto Ayacucho, which borders with Colombia. From there we hailed a pickup and made our way towards the community. Upon entering the indigenous community we were immediately greeted by the children in the village. It was obvious that the urban world had made its inroads into this village. Many of the people were dressed in non-traditional wear and some even lived in small concrete homes, in contrast to the palm-thatched homes. Despite the commonality in dress and some of the houses, I was immediately aware of the cultural differences from that of *Latinos*.

The boys from the Lighthouse Ranch (who had visited on a prior trip) immediately connected with some of the young people they already knew. As we made our way over to our home for the next few days, we set up our hammocks and organized ourselves. Over the next few days we helped with church services in the evening and work projects and games during the day. Due to the fact that there was no running water in town, baths were taken in a river. While some of the young people spoke Spanish all of the messages had to be translated into Piaröa.

Perhaps the most powerful aspect of this trip consisted in watching God use the boys from the Lighthouse Ranch. It really struck me on the way home on the bus, as I sat in the dark preparing to fall asleep, when one of the boys sat next to me and asked me to tell him my testimony. As I began to share my journey with the Lord it suddenly occurred to me that the dramatic transformation point in my life occurred when I was sixteen going on a short-term mission trip. It was at that point where God turned my life around. There was Michael, who is sixteen, on a short-term mission trip, being transformed himself. The difference is, Michael comes from a very difficult background. All of the boys on this trip were at one point "street children."

As I ponder this trip I am literally awe struck at how God works. Three boys, who use to live on the street, with very difficult backgrounds were used by God to minister in the Amazon! We serve a powerful God! Not only am I pleased to see God use these boys in such a great way, but it causes me to wonder if this is not one of the missing links to the rehabilitation of street dwelling children and other children at risk around the world. *"To love thy neighbor"* is probably one of the greatest intervention strategies we can offer these boys.

God finds great joy in using these boys and girls to reach people. As was mentioned, many of the girls that came out of the Door of Hope Mission in New York city were used by God as missionaries around the world. We can be sure that God desires to bring healing to children who are caught up living in desperate situations, but we should never underestimate to what extent the Lord will use these testimonies to reach out to many people from different walks of life.

AN UNREACHED PEOPLE GROUP?

Community children must be recognized for who they are, as God's children bearing His very own image. These girls and boys need to be taken seriously by the greater Church body. Children living on the street are "a large and rapidly growing unreached people group found on virtually all continents of our world" (Monsma 1993:1). As an unreached people group they deserve our emphasis. While God is moving among his people, there is still much to be accomplished. Monsma goes on to say, "If street children are a prominent unreached people group in cities, here is a group with millions of souls that has not yet been seriously addressed with the gospel" (1993:1). Yes, working with community children can be challenging, but if we are to have an impact we must think strategically and scrupulously.

In this movement we are called by God to reach millions of children and adolescents living on the street and not stop until all are won.

Dan Brewster has written and spoken about what he

calls the 4/14 window.[18] This movement of reaching community children and other children at risk for Christ is grounded not only in Biblical truth but in strategy as well. While there has been much attention given to the 10/40 window,[19] where most of the world's unreached people groups remain, little attention has been given to the 4/14 window of children at risk.

A few years ago, while I was preparing to go to Venezuela for the first time, I was confronted by another missionary who said that I should be going to a 10/40 window country for "real ministry." This missionary somehow felt that I would be more faithful to God if I would only go where the greatest need for evangelization (according to him) was located. I believe there is a tremendous need to work within the 10/40 window, but I also believe that there is another window. This window is the "biggest little mission field in the world" (Guthrie 1997:1).

Over one-third of the world's population fits in this 4/14 window and there are 1.8 billion children under the age of 15 with 1.5 billion of them in developing or third world countries. Dr. Bryant Myers, the director of World Vision's Urban Advance, tells us that in the USA 85% of people who make a decision for Christ, make it between the ages of 4 and 14 (Kilbourn 1996:126). That is why this 4/14 window is so important!

Dan Brewster describes this mission field as a "forgotten people group." He goes on to say, "What do we

---

18- The 4/14 window consists of children between the ages of 4 and 14, without Christ.

19- The 10/40 window is a belt that extends from west Africa across Asia, between ten degrees north of the equator to forty degrees north of the equator. This includes the Muslim, Hindu and Buddhist block countries.

have to say, from a missiological standpoint, to the poorest, most numerous, most disrupted, most hurting and possibly the most receptive of the world's population groups" (Kilbourn 1996:132). The fact is, many mission structures continue to say nothing, even in light of God's biblical basis for ministry.

As we look at modern mission agencies, many are interested in getting into and working within the 10/40 window. Many of these structures may find out that it will be through the 4/14 window that they actually have an impact. Reaching community children for Christ must be seen, in and of itself as important. We cannot allow the thought that children are only a means to reaching their parents. Unfortunately this idea, that children will help us reach others in the society has been suggested. This kind of reasoning is sinful (see James 2:1-4)! As Don Miller is quoted saying:

> I think we ought to minister to children because they are worthy of ministry, rather than to look at children as a vehicle to get to somebody else. That's a little manipulative . . . (Kilbourn 1997:234).

While reaching the 10/40 window is admirable, we must realize that reaching children in the street is just as important if we are to heed the call of God to reach all with the Gospel of Jesus Christ (Kilbourn 1996:137).

Yes, reaching community children is difficult, but so are other people groups around the world. Just as it is complex to reach Muslims so it will take strategy and research to win children living in the street to Christ. Many organizations have been raised up to see that Muslims are reached with the Gospel, so we must too, continue in mobilizing the Church to respond to the call of God to reach homeless and abandoned children in the name of Christ.

THE WAYS OF GOD

Several important aspects of this movement are: First, we see God working on the periphery, in the margins of society. God, in choosing to save boys and girls in the gutters of our world is declaring that He believes in them. While many people scoff at the thought that community children can be rehabilitated and used by God, the Father of the fatherless takes great pride in His creation and seeks to redeem them by His blood for a very special purpose. One remarkable detail is that we see "ex-street children" reaching out to those currently on the street; this is a pleasant surprise. Who would think that these boys and girls sleeping in the dark corners of the street would be raised up by God to be evangelists (e.g. Douglas and Marlon)? God is using youth, who at one point were seen by the world as "throwaways" and "trash," in a glorious way, as witnesses of His supremacy and mercy. Truly, the kingdom of God is up-side down in respect to our Lord's values and the values of the world!

A second aspect to this movement is the working of two structures. Most of the programs reaching out to community children are started by mission structures (e.g. World Vision, UFM International, Action International, *Niños de la Luz*, Latin America Mission, etc.). Normally, these mission structures work with churches in providing the children a place to worship and fellowship. In Caracas,

Niños de la Luz seeks to work alongside local churches by partnering in outreach. Often, the churches provide funds and personnel, with the NGO's providing the means for outreach. Churches and mission organizations must continue to work together for several reasons. First, because the world is watching us and waiting to see the unity of God's people. As NGO's and churches work hand in hand the kingdom of God is furthered. Secondly, Christian agencies and churches need each other. I was once told by a director of a ministry to community children, "but the churches simply don't want to work with us." They must find a way to work together.

Thirdly, a theological breakthrough is occurring in many circles around the world. Leaders are beginning to recognize the importance of children, especially children at risk. Strategies such as the 4/14 window and others emphasize this theological breakthrough. Consultations and meetings such as the Penang Consultation on Child Theology, the ASHA-Asia Consultation and Training on Sexual Abuse, the Cutting Edge conferences on children at risk, are providing the theological grounding needed for such a movement. Missionary leaders and pastors are using both New and Old Testament passages to emphasize care for orphans and other homeless children around the world. This must continue to take priority in our task of mobilization.

These are just a few of the ways we see God moving in a new way. God is at work in the lives of community children all over the world. This movement can be traced throughout Europe, the United States, Asia, Africa and Latin America. God continues to use unusual people in surprising ways. God is reaching children who sleep in dark corners and is raising them up to be examples of His grace. It is truly a privilege to be part of this movement of God.

9

A FINAL WORD

I hope and pray you sense better prepared, even challenged, to reach out and minister to some needy young people, not only in your own community, but cross-culturally as well. As we have seen, it is primarily the Church's responsibility to reach out to the homeless child and God enthusiastically loves to use His people to do it.

BEGIN WITH PRAYER

Our first desire is to gain God's perspective and to receive God's heart for neglected young people in our cities. Nouwen talks about the importance of prayer for the poor and neglected in his Latin American journal called, *Gracias!*:

> True prayer always includes becoming poor. When we pray we stand naked and vulnerable in front of our Lord

and show him our true condition. If one were to do this not just for oneself, but in the name of the thousands of surrounding poor people, wouldn't that be "mission" in the true sense of being sent into the world as Jesus himself was sent into the world? To lift up your hands to the Lord and show him the hungry children who play on the dust streets (1993:11).

To become poor through prayer, in our context, means that we must enter the painful reality of life on the street and feel what the children feel. Prayer is a tool of empathy, an empathy that goes beyond simply feeling bad for the victim. It's a state of weeping for the child and his or her situation. Surely God feels and suffers alongside many of these children. In order to gain God's perspective for these children we, and our churches, must start with prayer.

WALK IN THE SPIRIT

While many organizations are working with community children around the world, many do so relying on their own wisdom and energy. As Christians, what sets us apart is our dependence on the Holy Spirit. If we are to have an impact it will only come as a result of dependence on the Holy Spirit. Jesus himself relied upon the Holy Spirit in His ministry on earth (see Matthew 3:16, 17). How much more must we rely on the Spirit of God in our work? We should *"walk in the Spirit"* and be *"filled with the Spirit"*, as we are encouraged to in Galatians 5:16-26 and Ephesians 5:18 in order to minister in the power of the Spirit. Allow the Spirit of God to comfort you and to guide you, giving you wisdom as you go.

WHAT I HAVE LEARNED

My friends on the street and in police detention centers have taught me much about God and life. Nouwen has said, "true missioners are people who are hunting for the Divine treasure hidden in the heart of the people to whom they want to make the Good News known" (1993:19). To look for the "Divine treasure," is to look for the Messiah in these children. Christ is there, He's behind the dirt, the smell and the hardened responses we receive from many of the boys and girls. Christ is there and He is waiting to liberate His children!

What have I learned? I met Carlos a number of years ago. Carlos, has always had an incredible sense of compassion for others. He did not care for his own life all that much as far as I could tell, but he did show a great deal of concern for my life and that of others. On a number of circumstances he would tell me, "don't go there," or "be careful Greg." We have much to learn from children like Carlos.

Another boy who taught me about God was Edgar. He taught me about the unconditional love the Father shows toward those who are His own. Regardless of what Edgar would do he was always reminding me that Jesus loved him and cared about him. He knew that salvation did not come by works, but rather by God's love that was manifested at Calvary. Edgar never seemed to know what day it was or even the time, he lived each day as if it was his last. He lived Christ's command to not be concerned with tomorrow better than anyone I have ever known.

May you, as you prepare to serve the community child, or in your current ministry never forget to seek after the "Divine treasure" that God has placed in the hearts of those children and youth you have been called to reach. May we get beyond the thought that, 'these kids need us,' to, 'we need these children and youth' in the kingdom of God. God desires to see every child who has been thrown out of their home and abandoned, transformed into children of the King who will radically change the current unjust systems and structures that have put them where they are. God wants to employ these children as powerful reminders to the world of His tremendous love and grace.

God has given us the tools and the means to reach these boys and girls with the Gospel. Jesus Christ and His death on the cross has provided the bridge to eternal life, no matter how far we have drifted from our Creator. We can be certain that God will enable us with the authority and mercy to go forward with our ministries to them, for we serve a God of hope and restoration.

As we go and minister, in the name of Jesus, may we go with His love for these children. May we learn to love as the Father loves and may we go in the power of the Spirit of God, ever mindful that the Lord of Hosts has gone before us and is preparing the way.

I absolutely love this saying from this early church father, and I would like to conclude with it:

> *[Community children] are said to be the rag, tag and bobtail of humanity. But Jesus does not leave them that way. Out of material you would have thrown away as useless, he fashions [people of strength], giving them back their self-respect, enabling them to stand on their feet and look God in the eye. They were cowed, cringing, broken things. But the Son has set them free!* Origen (3rd Century A.D.)

BIBLIOGRAPHY

* ANDERSON, JEFF
  – 1995 Crisis on the Streets: A Manual for Ministry to Street Children. Manila, Philippines: Action Publishing.

* ANDERSON, NEIL T.
  – 1990 The Bondage Breaker. Eugene, OR: Harvest House.

* APTEKAR, LEWIS
  – 1988 Street Children of Cali. Durham: Duke University Press.

* ATKINS, ANDY AND GRAHAM GORDON
  – 1999 "Advocacy Study pack." Tearfund Case Study Series.

* BEAUNAUX, JAMES
  –1993 "Children at Risk." Evangelical Missions Quarterly 29(4): 374-379.

* BYRNE, IAIN
  – 1998 The Human Rights of Street and Working Children: A Practical Manual for Advocates. London: Intermediate Technology Publications LTD.

* CHAPMAN, GARY AND ROSS CAMPBELL
  – 1997 The Five Love Languages of Children. Chicago, IL: Moody Publishers.

* COCKBURN, ANNETTE
  – 1991 "Street children: An overview of the extent, causes, characteristics and dynamics of the problem." The Child Care Worker 9(1): 12-13.

- CONN, HARVIE M. AND MANUEL ORTIZ
  - 2001 Urban Ministry. The Kingdom, the City and the People of God. Downers Grove, IL: IVP.

- COSGROVE, JOHN G.
  - –1990 "Towards a working definition of street children." International Social Work 33:185-192.

- COSTA, ORLANDO E.
  - –1974 The Church and its Mission: A Shattering Critique from the Third World. Wheaton, IL: Tyndale.

- DE CARVALHO, SARAH
  - – 1996 The Street Children of Brazil. London: Hodder & Stoughton.

- DODD, CARLEY H.
  - – 1998 Dynamics of Intercultural Communication. Boston, MA: McGraw Hill.

- ENNEW, JUDITH
  - – 2000 Street and Working Children: A Guide to Planning. London: Save the Children.

- FELSMAN, JACKSON
  - – 1982 "Street Urchins of Cali: On Risk, Resiliency and Adaptation in Childhood." Ph.D. dissertation, Harvard University.

- FYNN, MIKE AND DOUG GREGG
  - – 1993 Inner Healing. Downers Grove, IL: IVP.

- GOTT, RICHARD
  - – 2000 In the Shadow of the Liberator: The Impact of Hugo Chavez on Venezuela and Latin America. London: Verso.

- GRANT, JAMES P.
  - – 1992 "Improving the Lives of Street Children," Lecture. Rio de Janeiro, Brazil: Second International Conference on Street Youth.

- GREENWAY, ROGER, EDITOR.
  –1980 Discipling the City: Theological Reflections on Urban Mission. Grand Rapids, MI: Baker.

- GREENWAY, ROGER AND TIMOTHY MONSMA
  – 1989 Cities: Missions' New Frontier. Grand Rapids, MI: Baker.

- GROVE, JOHN G.
  – 1990 "Towards a working definition of street children" International Social Work 33:185-192.

- GRUNLAN, STEPHEN A. AND MARVIN MAYERS
  – 1988 Cultural Anthropology. Grand Rapids, MI: Zondervan.

- GUTHRIE, DONALD
  – 1981 New Testament Theology. Downers Grove, IL: IVP.

- GUTHRIE, STAN
  – 1997 "Children at Risk." World Pulse 32(24): 1-2.

- HAUGEN, GARY A.
  – 1999 Good News about Injustice. Downers Grove, IL: IVP.

- HECHT, TOBIAS
  – 1998 At Home in the Street. New York, NY: Cambridge.

- HESTER, CLARE
  – 2000 "Mission Impossible: Rescuing children from the street." Hope for Children in Crisis. Nov.-Jan., Vol.2, No.2.

- HUGHES, DEWI
  – 1998 God of the Poor. Cumbria, UK: OM Publishing.

- IRVINE, GRAEME
  – 1991 "Abandoned Children, The Most Marginalized." Together, World Vision International Journal: October-December, 1991.

- JOHNSTONE, PATRICK
  - 1993 Operation World. Grand Rapids, MI: Zondervan.

- KILBOURN, PHYLLIS, EDITOR.
  - 1997 Street Children: A Guide to Effective Ministry. Monrovia, CA: MARC.
  - 1996 Children in Crisis: A New Commitment. Monrovia, CA: MARC.

- KILBOURN, PHYLLIS AND MARJORIE McDERMAID, EDITORS.
  - 1998 Sexually Exploited Children: Working to Protect and Heal. Monrovia, CA: MARC.

- KRAFT, CHARLES H.
  - 1991 Communication Theory for Christian Witness. Maryknoll, NY: Orbis.

- KRAYBILL, DONALD B.
  - 1978 The Upside-Down Kingdom. Scottsdale, PA: Herald Press.

- LADD, GEORGE ELDON
  - 1959 The Gospel of the Kingdom. Grand Rapids, MI: Eerdmans.

- LINTHICUM, ROBERT C.
  - 1991 City of God, City of Satan. Grand Rapids, MI: Zondervan.
  - 1991 Empowering the Poor. Monrovia, CA: MARC.

- LUSK, MARK W.
  - 1989 "Street Children Programs in Latin America." Journal of Sociology & Social Welfare 16 (1): 55-77.

- LUSK, MARK W. AND IRENE RIZZINI
  - 1993 "Children in the Streets: Latin America's Lost Generation" Children and Youth Services Review 17 (3):391-400.

- LUSK, MARK W., FELIPE PERALTA AND GERALD W. VEST
  - 1989 "Street Children of Juarez: a field study" International Social Work 32:289-302.

- MÁRQUEZ, PATRICIA CAROL
  - 1995 "Youth on the Streets, Commodities, and violence in Caracas." Ph.D. dissertation, University of California at Berkeley.
- MILES, GLENN AND JOSEPHINE-JOY WRIGHT, EDITORS
  - 2003 Celebrating Children: Equipping people working with children and young people living in difficult circumstances around the world. Cumbria, UK: Partnoster Press.

- MONSMA, TIMOTHY
  - 1993 "The Rehabilitation of Street Children; Case Studies from Manila." City Watch 8 (4):1-3
  - 1989 "...But the workers are few." City Watch 4 (1):1-2.

- NOUWEN, HENRI J.M.
  - 1993 Gracias. New York: Orbis Books.
  - 1989 In the Name of Jesus. New York, NY: Crossroads.

- OTIS, GEORGE
  - 1991 The Last of the Giants. Grand Rapids, MI: Chosen.

- PERKINS, JOHN
  - 1993 Beyond Charity: The Call to Christian Community Development. Grand Rapids, MI: Baker.

- PIPER, JOHN
  - 1997 A Godward Life. Portland, OR: Multnomah.

- RAFFAELLI, MARCELA
  - 1997 "The family situation of street youth in Latin America: a cross-national review." International Social Work 40:89-100.

- ROUX, JOHANN LE AND CHERYL SYLVIA SMITH
  - 1998 "Psychological Characteristics of South African Street Children." Adolescence 33 (132): 891-900
  - 1998 "Public Perceptions of, and Reactions to, Street Children." Adolescence 33 (132): 901-914
  - 1998 "Is the Street Child Phenomenon Synonymous with Deviant Behavior?" Adolescence 33 (132): 915-924.

- SCANLON, THOMAS, ANDREW TOMSKINS, MARGARET LYNCH AND FRANCESCA SCANLON
  - 1998 "Street Children in Latin America." British Medical Journal 316 (7144): 1596-1607.

- SEAMANDS, DAVID
  - 1985 Healing of Memories. Wheaton: Victor.

- SIDER, RONALD J.
  - 1997 Rich Christians in an Age of Hunger. Dallas, TX: WORD
  - 1993 One Sided Christianity? Grand Rapids, MI: Zondervan.

- SOARES, ZENI DE LIMA
  - 1996 "Children: A permanent challenge to the churches." International Review of Mission vol. 85 (338):427-446.

- TABER, CHARLES R.
  - 2002 "In the Image of God: The Gospel and Human Rights." International Bulletin of Missionary Research. July 2002.

- TIERNEY, NANCY LEIGH
  - 1997 Robbed of Humanity: Lives of Guatemalan Street Children. Saint Paul: Pangaea.

- TUCKER, RUTH
  - 1992 Guardians of the Great Commission. Grand Rapids, MI: Academie Books.

- TURNER, SHARLEEN
  - 1992 "Long Road for Street Kids." Latin America Evangelist. October-December, pages 10-11.

- VINCENT, DAVID
  - 1995 "The Street Children of Quelimane, Mozambique." City Watch 10 (2):1-4.

- VIVA NETWORK
  - 2000 "Tool Kit." Reaching Children at Risk 4 (2):14

- WAGNER, PETER C.
  –1992 Warfare Prayer. Ventura, CA: Regal Books.
  –1991 Engaging the Enemy. Ventura, CA: Regal Books.

- WAGNER, PETER C. AND DOUGLAS PENNOYER
  –1990 Wrestling With Dark Angels: Toward a Deeper Understanding of the Supernatural Forces in Spiritual Warfare. Ventura, CA: Regal Books.

- WALLIS, JIM
  –1981 The Call to Conversion: Recovering the Gospel for these Times. San Francisco, CA: Harper and Row.

- WILLARD, DALLAS
  – 1988 The Spirit of the Disciplines. New York, NY: Harper San Francisco.

- WINK, WALTER
  –1992 Engaging the Powers. Minneapolis, MN: Fortress.

- WORLD VISION
  –1992 Children and Violence. Federal Way, WA: World Vision.